Elihu Samuel Riley

Celebration of the Two Hundredth Anniversary of the Removal

of the Capital of Maryland from St. Mary's to Annapolis, March 5, 1894

Elihu Samuel Riley

Celebration of the Two Hundredth Anniversary of the Removal
of the Capital of Maryland from St. Mary's to Annapolis, March 5, 1894

ISBN/EAN: 9783337236847

Printed in Europe, USA, Canada, Australia, Japan

Cover: Foto ©ninafisch / pixelio.de

More available books at **www.hansebooks.com**

MEMORIAL VOLUME.

CELEBRATION

OF THE

TWO HUNDREDTH ANNIVERSARY

OF THE

REMOVAL OF THE CAPITAL

OF

MARYLAND

FROM ST. MARY'S TO ANNAPOLIS.

MARCH 5, 1894.

Edited by ELIHU S. RILEY,

Under the Authority of the House of Delegates of Maryland,
of 1894.

ANNAPOLIS:
KING BROS., STATE PRINTERS
1894.

PREFACE.

This volume is not only the memorial of the celebration of the two hundredth anniversary of the removal of the Capital from St. Mary's to Annapolis, but it is the natural outgrowth of those interesting and profitable ceremonies. It was the expressed thought, almost from the moment the attention of the General Assembly was called to the subject of the celebration, that the papers, written for the occasion, should be preserved in a substantial form. In this, the Maryland Legislature of 1894 expurgates itself from the standing indictment that Marylanders, with a proud and noble history, have been culpably indifferent to preserving the records of it, and in transmitting to posterity, unimpaired, these sources of wisdom and inspiration to heroic deeds and righteous government.

By the accidents of legislation, the work of inaugurating and consummating, on the part of the General Assembly, fell chiefly to the House of Delegates. From the inception of the movement to the close of the proceedings, the city of Annapolis and St. John's College had the intelligent and cordial assistance of THOMAS S.

Baer, Esq., Chairman of the House Committee on Public Records, to which committee the House had delegated its part of the work of preparation. The chairman was seconded, in absolute unanimity, by every member of the committee, in each portion of the programme. It is no invidious distinction, on the part of the editor of this volume, to say that, if the incidental data and historical papers of this work are worth preserving, then the State is indebted particularly to the enthusiastic and intelligent encouragement that Messrs. A. FREDERICK GEORGE and TILGHMAN J. FAHRNEY, members of the House Committee on Public Records, gave to the compiler, in the initiatory, steps to bring, to the attention of the House, the propriety of printing a memorial of the celebration.

J. HEMSLEY JOHNSON, Esq., of the same committee, mover of the resolution to print, was one of the earliest advocates of the memorial volume, and the unanimity of the House upon the subject was a compliment to the patriotic grasp which the author of the order had on the vital subject of the preservation, and diffusion of our records to the people of the State.

The neat typography entirely, and, in many cases, the artistic arrangement of the subjects in book form, is due to the skill and quick perceptions of the competent State Printers, Messrs. KING BROS., of Baltimore.

PREFACE.

May the facts here gathered inspire all Marylanders with a deeper love and better work for our own Commonwealth, and may other States of our most glorious Union catch, as in the past, inspiration from the history of a colony which wrought for God and man alike.

ELIHU S. RILEY.

ANNAPOLIS, March 19, 1894.

CONTENTS.

	PAGE
Maryland Legislature of 1694...	1
Maryland Legislature of 1894	3
Inauguration of the Celebration	11
Commissioners of Annapolis in 1694	20
Corporation of Annapolis in 1894	20
Officers of the City of Annapolis, 1894	21
Committees of Arrangement, 1894	22
Meeting of Citizens of Annapolis	23
Invitation of Citizens' Meeting	26
Card to Citizens	27
Official Program	27
The Day	30
The Street Parade	31
Masquerade, Illumination and Ball	35
On the part of St. John's College	36
On the part of the City of Annapolis and State of Maryland	38
King William's School	40
Board of Visitors and Governors of St. John's College	43
The Faculty of St. John's College	44
Prayer of Rev. H. H. Clarke	45
Address by Gen. H. Kyd Douglas	47
Address by James W. Thomas	62
Prayer by Rev. W. S. Southgate	84
Remarks by Thomas S. Baer	86
Address by Elihu S. Riley	89
Address by Alfred P. Dennis	118
Letters	146
Annapolis in 1694	159
Annapolis in 1894	165
Notes, Incidents, Thanks	168

MARYLAND LEGISLATURE OF 1694,

AT ANNAPOLIS

THE GOVERNOR AND COUNCIL.

UPPER HOUSE.

FRANCIS NICHOLSON, Governor.

Col. NICHOLAS GREENBERRY,
Col. GEORGE ROBOTHAM,
EDWARD RANDOLPH,
Col. JOHN ADDISON,
JAMES FRISBY,
THOMAS BROOKE,
                          Councillors.

HOUSE OF BURGESSES, OR LOWER HOUSE.

For the City of St. Mary's.
Capt. THOS. WANGHOP.

For St. Mary's County.

Mr. KENELM CHISELYDINE,   Mr. ROBERT MASON,
Mr. PHILIP CLARKE,   Capt. JOHN BAYNE.

For Kent County.

Coll. HANS HANSON,   Mr. JOHN HINSON,
Mr. WILLIAM FRISBY,   Mr. THOMAS SMITH.

Maryland Legislature of 1694—Continued

For Calvert County.
Mr. GEORGE LOUGHAM,   Mr. THOMAS TASKER.

For Ann Arundel County.
Capt. JOHN HAMMOND,   Mr. JOHN SANDERS,
Maj. EDWARD DORSEY.

For Charles County.
Mr. HY. HAWKINS,   Coll. JAS. SMALLWOOD,
Col. WILLIAM DENT.

For Baltimore County.
Mr. EDWARD BROOKBY,   Mr. FRANCIS WATKINS,
Mr. JOHN FERRY.

For Talbot County.
Mr. ROBERT SMITH,   Col. HENRY COURSEY,
Mr. THOMAS SMITHSON.

For Dorchester County.
Mr. JOHN POLLARD,   Mr. THOMAS HICKS,
Mr. THOMAS ENNALS.

For Cecil County.
Col. CASPERUS A. HERMAN,   Coll. WILLIAM PEERCE.

1894.

GOVERNOR:
HON. FRANK BROWN.

SECRETARY OF STATE:
HON. WILLIAM T. BRANTLY.

LIST OF MEMBERS AND OFFICERS
OF THE
GENERAL ASSEMBLY OF MARYLAND.
JANUARY SESSION, 1894.

SENATORS.

ALLEGANY COUNTY.
James M. Sloan..........Merchant..........Lonaconing.

ANNE ARUNDEL COUNTY.
Robert Moss.............Ed. and Lawyer...Annapolis.

BALTIMORE COUNTY.
John Hubner.............Builder...........Catonsville.

BALTIMORE CITY.
First District.
Charles H. Evans...   ....Printer and Pub..1710 E. Chase.

Second District.
Wm. Cabell Bruce........Lawyer... ....Equitable Building.

Third District.
Thomas G. Hayes.........Lawyer...........Equitable Building.

MARYLAND LEGISLATURE OF 1894—Continued.

CALVERT COUNTY.
Thomas Parran............Farmer.........St. Leonard's.

CAROLINE COUNTY.
Thomas A. Smith.........Farmer..........Ridgely.

CARROLL COUNTY.
Pinkney J. Bennett......Farmer..........Westminster.

CECIL COUNTY.
Charles C. Crothers.......Lawyer...........Elkton.

CHARLES COUNTY.
Lewis C. Carrico...........Farmer and Phys..Hughesville

DORCHESTER COUNTY
Joseph H. Johnson........Lawyer...........Cambridge.

FREDERICK COUNTY.
Jacob M. Newman........Merchant.........Frederick.

GARRETT COUNTY.
Robert A. Ravenscroft... Physician.........Accident.

HARFORD COUNTY.
William S. Baker..........Fruit Packer......Aberdeen.

HOWARD COUNTY.
John G. Rogers............Lawyer...........Ellicott City.

KENT COUNTY.
Wm. T. Hepbron......... Farmer...........Kennedyville.

MONTGOMERY COUNTY.
Hattersly W. Talbott......Lawyer...........Rockville.

PRINCE GEORGE'S COUNTY.
William D. Bowie........Farmer...........Collington.

QUEEN ANNE'S COUNTY.
Woodland P. Finley.......Farmer...........Church Hill.

MARLYAND LEGISLATURE OF 1894—*Continued.*

ST. MARY'S COUNTY.
Washington Wilkinson....Merchant........Holly Wood.

SOMERSET COUNTY.
Levin L. Waters.........Lawyer...........Princess Anne.

TALBOT COUNTY.
Oswald Tilghman.........Lawyer..........Easton.

WASHINGTON COUNTY.
David Seibert............Farmer ....Clear Spring.

WICOMICO COUNTY.
E. Stanley Toadvin.......Lawyer..........Salisbury.

WORCESTER COUNTY.
John Walter Smith...... { Bank Pres't and / Lumber Manf... } Snow Hill.

OFFICERS OF THE SENATE.

JOHN WALTER SMITH, - - *President.*

JAMES ROGER McSHERRY,	FRANK SHIPLEY,
Secretary.	*Journal Clerk.*
WILLIAM I. HILL,	WM. H. RICHARDSON,
Reading Clerk.	*Sergeant-at-Arms.*

HOUSE OF DELEGATES.

ALLEGANY COUNTY.
Jos. B. Stottlemeyer...... Farmer..........Little Orleans.
William Sleeman.........Miner ....Vale Summit.
John H. Shuck...........Painter ....Cumberland.
Hugh McMillan..........Miner ....Frostburg.
John H. Jones...........R. R. Employee...Westernport.

MARYLAND LEGISLATURE OF 1894—Continued.

ANNE ARUNDEL COUNTY.

James R. Brashears	Lawyer	Annapolis.
Geo. M. Murray	Pack. and Truck	Odenton.
Chas. F. Sappington	Farmer	Welham's X Roads.
Geo. W. Hyde	Farmer	Galloway.

BALTIMORE CITY.

First Legislative District.

Geo. E. Keenan	Attorney-at-Law	315 Law Building.
Edward D. Fitzgerald	Attorney-at-Law	Daily Record Bldg.
Joseph W. Hazell	Attorney-at-Law	213 Courtland st.
Geo. A. Vernetson	Merchant	138 Aisquith.
W. H. B. Fusselbaugh, of J.	Merchant	422 N. Gay.
Samuel E. Atkinson		18 N. Chester.

Second Legislative District.

Thomas S. Baer	Lawyer	208 Courtland.
Charles H. Carter	Lawyer	Lex'n and Charles.
Archibald H. Taylor	Lawyer	104 E. Lexington.
Charles W. Field	Lawyer	Farmers' and Merchants' Bldg.
John Hemsley Johnson	Lawyer	236 Courtland.
Jas. H. Preston, *Speaker*	Lawyer	220 St. Paul.

Third Legislative District.

Dan'l W. Stubbs	Carpenter	111 Hanover.
Henry Hasenkamp	Merchant	623 W. Lee.
Joseph P. McGonigle	Manufacturer	204 E. Randall.
Philip Singleton	Merchant	1201 Ridgely.
W. D. Robinson	Lawyer	839 N. Fremont.
John F. Williams	Lawyer	24 Lexington.

MARYLAND LEGISLATURE OF 1894—*Continued*.

BALTIMORE COUNTY.

James B. Councilman	Farmer	Mt. Wilson.
John C. Bosley	Farmer	Shawan.
Frederick S. Myerly	School teacher	Black Rock.
Osborne I. Yellott	Lawyer	Towson.
George S. Keiffer	Book-keeper	Mt. Winans.
Thomas G. Carter	Farmer	Gardenville.

CALVERT COUNTY.

William H. Dowell	Farmer	Sheridan's Point.
Wallace Owings	Farmer	1128 N. Fulton ave., Balto.

CAROLINE COUNTY.

Henry R. Lewis	Lawyer	Denton.
Albert W. Sisk	Broker	Preston.

CARROLL COUNTY.

Johnzie E. Beasman	Farm. and Dairy	Sykesville.
Benjamin F. Selby	Farmer	Watersville.
John W. Biggs	Farmer	
Noah Sullivan	Farmer	Manchester.

CECIL COUNTY.

Geo. S. Woolley		Chesapeake City.
Frank H. Mackie	Physician	Fair Hill.
Richard L. Thomas	Merchant	Northeast.

CHARLES COUNTY.

James A. Franklin	Civil Engineer	Pisgah.
John E. Stone	Lawyer	La Plata.

MARYLAND LEGISLATURE OF 1894—*Continued.*

DORCHESTER COUNTY.

Francis P. Phelps	Fruit grower	Mt. Holly.
Wm. F. Applegarth	Merchant	Golden Hill.
Levi D. Travers	Banker	Cambridge.

FREDERICK COUNTY.

Melvin P. Wood	Merchant	New Market.
John R. Rouzer	Farmer	Thurmont.
James P. Perry		Frederick.
Andrew A. Annan	Farmer	Emmittsburg.
Geo. W. Crum, Jr.	Farmer	Lander.

GARRETT COUNTY.

A. Frederick George	Carp. and Builder	Swanton.
J. George Kolb	Carp. and Lumber Mfgr	Friendsville.

HARFORD COUNTY.

Samuel S. Bevard	Farmer	Emmerton.
Harold Scarboro	Lawyer	Belair.
Thomas B. Hayward	Physician	Clairmount Mills.
John O. Stearns	Farmer	Whiteford.

HOWARD COUNTY.

Louis P. Haslup	Manufacturer	Annapolis Junct.
Humphrey D. Wolfe	Farmer	Glenwood.

KENT COUNTY.

Enoch G. Clark	Phys. and Farm.	Millington.
Thomas R. Strong	Farmer	Eadsville.

Maryland Legislature of 1894—*Continued.*

Montgomery County.

Elisha C. Etchison	Physician	Gaithersburg.
Wm. H. Lamar	Lawyer	Rockville.
Robert M. Mackall	Farmer	Olney.

Prince George's County.

George M. Smith	Farm. and Merch.	Bowie.
Joseph S. Wilson	Attorney-at-Law	Upper Marlboro.
Dent Downing	Teacher	Aquasco.

Queen Anne's County.

Wm. Henry Legg	Real Estate Agt.	Centreville.
John O. Phillips	Justice of Peace	Chester.
Charles W. Clements	Merchant	Crumpton.

St. Mary's County.

Wm. F. Chesley	Farmer	Charlotte Hall.
John S. Jones	Farmer	Jarboesville.

Somerset County.

Oliver P. Byrd	Oyster Dealer	Crisfield.
Wm. A. Tull	Merchant	Marion.
Philetus N. Cannon	Merchant	Monie.

Talbot County.

Ormond Hammond	Farmer and General Agent	Royal Oak.
William Collins	Farmer	La Trappe.
Francis G. Wrightson	Farmer	Sherwood.

MARYLAND LEGISLATURE OF 1894—Continued.

WASHINGTON COUNTY.

Norman B. Scott, Jr.	Lawyer.	Hagerstown.
John H. Harp.	Farmer	Chewsville.
Tilghman J. Fahrney.	Merchant	Downsville.
Jeremiah B. Cromer.	Farmer	Hagerstown.

WICOMICO COUNTY.

Thomas S. Roberts.	Farmer	Capitola.
Albert W. Robinson.	Manufacturer	Sharptown.
Ebenezer G. Davis.	Merchant	New Hope.

WORCESTER COUNTY.

Lloyd Wilkinson.	Lawyer	Pocomoke City.
Jerome T. Hayman.	Farm. and Merch	Eden.
Peter Whaley.	Merchant	Whaleyville.

OFFICERS.

JAMES H. PRESTON, - - *Speaker.*

BENJAMIN L. SMITH, *Chief Clerk.*

WILLIAM S. MERRICK, *Journal Clerk.*

WALTER R. TOWNSEND, *Reading Clerk.*

JOSEPH T. C. KENLY, *Sergeant-at-Arms.*

JOHN R. SULLIVAN, *Chief Janitor,* - - Annapolis, Md.

JOHN S. KELLY, *Chief Doorkeeper,* - - Baltimore City.

KING BROTHERS, Baltimore, Md., *State Printers.*

The Inauguration of the Celebration.

ON the 12th of October, 1893, at a regular session of the City Council of Annapolis, City Counsellor Elihu S. Riley offered the following preamble and resolution:

WHEREAS, The two hundredth anniversary of the removal of the Capital of the State to Annapolis will occur on March 12th, 1894;

Resolved, That the Mayor appoint a committee of three, of which he shall be chairman, to take such steps as will properly celebrate this important historic event, and that the Legislature be requested to join in appropriately noticing an occurrence that marked such signal changes in the political and commercial history of the State.

The preamble and resolution were unanimously adopted, and the following committee, in accordance therewith, was appointed: Mayor John H. Thomas, Chairman, City Counsellor Elihu S. Riley, and Alderman Charles G. Feldmeyer.

At a meeting of the committee, it was resolved that the Legislature of 1894, January Session, be requested to participate in the celebration, and to appoint an orator to deliver an address on the occasion of the celebration. It was further resolved that Elihu S. Riley be appointed to act as historiographer of the Removal; Charles G. Feldmeyer be made musical director of the program of celebration; Frank B. Mayer, superintendent of a histrionic pageant to represent the event.

It was subsequently resolved to invite St. John's College to participate in the event, since the initiatory legislation to establish King William's School, the progenitor of St. John's College, was begun in 1694, the year the capital was removed to Annapolis.

The College and the gentlemen assigned to their several parts in the program of exercises, severally accepted the positions and parts allotted to them.

On January 9th, 1894, the committee of the City Council of Annapolis, through Delegate James R. Brashears of Anne Arundel county, submitted the following petition:

ANNAPOLIS, January 9th, 1894.

To the Honorable Speaker, President of the Senate and Members of the General Assembly:

Your memorialists respectfully represent that they have been appointed a committee of the City Council of Annapolis, to provide for the proper celebration of the two hundredth anniversary of the removal of the Capital from St. Mary's to Annapolis, which occurs March 5th, 1894; that the said City Council also requested in its resolution that the Legislature of the State take part in said ceremonies; that the said committee of the City Council has selected Frank B. Mayer to formulate and take charge of a histrionic pageant suitable to the occasion; that it has chosen Elihu S. Riley, as the historiographer of said event, and has appointed Charles G. Feldmeyer to direct the musical part of the ceremonies; that the said committee has invited the authorities of the St. John's College to be represented, by reason of the inauguration in 1694, of its progenitor, King William's School, in the celebration, and the said committee respectfully requests that the General Assembly will select an orator to represent said body on so memorable an occasion.

Very respectfully submitted,
JOHN H. THOMAS,
Mayor.
ELIHU S. RILEY,
CHAS. G. FELDMEYER.

This invitation was referred to the Committee on Public Records, consisting of the following members:

MESSRS. THOMAS S. BAER, of Baltimore City.
JAMES R. BRASHEARS, of Anne Arundel County.
HAROLD SCARBORO, of Harford County.
NORMAN B SCOTT, JR., of Washington County.
GEORGE E. KEENAN, of Baltimore City.
JOHN O. PHILLIPS, of Queen Anne's County.
TILGHMAN J. FAHRNEY, of Washington County.
A. FREDERICK GEORGE, of Garrett County.
JOHN HEMSLEY JOHNSON, of Baltimore City.

The committee, on the 18th of January, met, by appointment, the committee of the City Council, represented by Elihu S. Riley and Charles G. Feldmeyer, and the committee on the part of St. John's College, represented by Dr. Thomas Fell, president of St. John's College. Mr. Riley presented the proposed celebration on the part of the city of Annapolis, and Dr. Thomas Fell, for St. John's College. The committee of the House, after the retirement of the gentlemen from Annapolis city and St. John's College, had a meeting, and unanimously resolved to accept the invitation given to the Legislature, and further resolved to send the subjoined message by the House of Delegates to the Senate, which was done that day. Mr. Baer offered the message.

BY THE HOUSE OF DELEGATES,

January 18th, 1894.

Gentlemen of the Senate:

We have received from John H. Thomas, Mayor of Annapolis, and others, a memorial, requesting the General Assembly to participate in a proposed celebration on March 5th, 1894, of the two hundredth anniversary of the removal of the Capital of the State from St. Mary's to Annapolis, by the selection of an orator to represent the General Assembly on that occasion, which memorial has been referred to the Committee on Public Records, and is annexed to this message. We request the Senate to refer the matter to a committee to co-operate with the said committee of the House of Delegates in the consideration of said memorial.

By order,

B. L. SMITH,
Chief Clerk.

Which was adopted by the House.

The Senate responded with the following message, offered by Mr. Hayes:

By The Senate,

January 22d, 1894.

Gentlemen of the House of Delegates:

We have received your message, with memorial attached, requesting the General Assembly to participate in a proposed celebration on March 5th, 1894, of the two hundredth anniversary of its removal of the Capital of the State from St. Mary's to Annapolis, by the selection of an orator to represent the General Assembly on that occasion, and we concur therein. The Senate has appointed Messrs. Hayes, Tilghman, Parran, Wilkinson and Moss to act jointly with your Committee of Public Records.

By order,

J. ROGER McSHERRY,

Secretary.

Subsequently, the two committees, thus appointed, met in joint session, and unanimously agreed to invite Prof. Alfred Pearce Dennis, of Princeton College, a native of Worcester county, Maryland, to make the address on the part of the House. This invitation was duly accepted.

The committee, on the part of the City Council of Annapolis, also asked James W. Thomas, Esq., of Cumberland, who had devoted considerable time to the subject, to read a paper on "St. Mary's City." This invitation Mr. Thomas accepted.

Adj.-General H. Kyd Douglas was invited by the committee on the part of St. John's College to represent that institution in the celebration. This invitation was accepted. Mr. Thomas was assigned by the committee of the City Council to read his paper in St. John's College part of the program.

In the House of Delegates, Tuesday, February 27, on motion of Mr. Baer, it was—

Ordered, That the use of the hall of the House of Delegates, on the evening of Monday, March 5th, be granted to the Mayor and City Council of Annapolis, for the celebration of the two hundredth anniversary of the removal of the Capital of the State from St. Mary's to Annapolis.

In the House of Delegates, Thursday, March 1st, on motion of Mr. Baer, it was—

Ordered, That the Superintendent of Public Buildings be directed to remove the desks from the hall of the House of Delegates on the evening of the 5th of March, and return the same to their places by 10 A. M., of the following morning, and that the floor and the arrangement of the seats upon the occasion, be under the control of the Speaker of the House, the President of the Senate and the Joint and Special Committees of the two Houses, on the celebration of the two hundredth anniversary of the removal of the capital.

Mr. Johnson submitted the following order:

Ordered, That the Committee on Claims pay to the Hon. John H. Thomas, Mayor of Annapolis, the sum of $250, to be applied to the defraying the expenses of the celebration of the two hundredth anniversary of the transfer of the State Capital to Annapolis.

Which was read and referred to the Committee on Claims, and on Friday, March 2, was favorably reported from the said committee, and the order was adopted by the House.

On Thursday, March 1st, Mr. Johnson submitted the following order:

Ordered, That Elihu S. Riley be and he is hereby requested to edit and prepare for publication a memorial volume of the celebration of the two hundredth anniversary of the removal of the Capital from St. Mary's to Annapolis, said volume to contain the proceedings of the two Houses of the Legislature on the subject, and the several papers in full to be read on the part of St. John's College, the city of Annapolis and the State of Maryland, on March 5, and the Printing Committee of the House of Delegates is hereby directed to have printed before the 21st of March, instant, one thousand copies of the same, 250 copies to be bound in cloth, and 750 to be bound in paper, to be distributed by the Committee on Public Records as follows: One hundred copies, bound in cloth, to the State Library; five copies, one of which shall be bound in cloth, to each of the Senators and members of the House of Delegates, for public distribution; one hundred copies to St. John's College, twenty to be bound in cloth; twenty-five copies, one of which shall be in cloth, to each of the speakers at the celebration; five copies to each of the members of the Joint Committee of the two Houses having the celebration in charge, and the balance to be distributed in the discretion of said Joint Committee.

That said Riley be paid the sum of three hundred dollars for editing said work, and that the State Printer be paid therefor at the rate now allowed him by law for public printing.

Which was read, and referred to the Committee on Public Records.

On March 7, the Committee on Public Records made a favorable report on the above order, with the amendment that the said Riley be paid the sum of $250 for editing the volume.

The order was adopted by the House by the following vote:

AFFIRMATIVE—Messrs. Speaker, Chesley, Jones of St. Mary's, Strong, Brashears, Murray, Sappington, Hyde, Dowell, Franklin, Councilman, Bosley, Myerly, Kieffer, Carter of Baltimore county, Hammond, Wrightson, Byrd, Cannon, Phelps, Travers, Woodley, Mackie, Smith, Wilson, Legg, Clements, Wilkinson, Hayman, Wood, Rouzer, Perry, Annan, Crum, Jr., Scarboro, Stearns, Lewis, Sisk, Keenan, Vernetson, Atkinson, Baer, Carter of Baltimore city, Taylor, Johnson, Hasenkamp, Singleton, Scott, Jr., Fahrney, Mackall, Stottlemyer, Sleeman, Shuck, McMillan, Jones of Allegany, Beasman, Biggs, Sullivan, Wolfe, Kolb.—61.

NEGATIVE—Messrs. Bevard, Harp, Davis.—3.

It will be observed that the date of the resolution passed in the City Council of Annapolis, was to celebrate the 12th of March, and the memorial to the Legislature names the 5th. This was a divergence that made no essential difference, as an exact date would vary as different minds looked at the events.

The original proceedings of removal are recorded as having taken place in the House at St. Mary's, on October 11th, 1694, and the assembly is stated to have met at Annapolis on February 28th, 1694. (Old style.) It was at a time when dates were written two ways, but it is undoubtedly so that it was on February 28th, 1694, (old style), the Assembly first met in Annapolis. If we omit the eleven days added by the change of dates from old style to new, it would make the day of meeting here March 11th; but the records reached Annapolis before that date, no doubt, so as to be ready for the Legislature. So there are three dates by which the celebration might readily be noted: October 11th, 1693, instead of 1694, as found in the record; the unknown day on which the records arrived in the winter of 1694; and the 11th of March, 1694, when the Legislature first assembled at Annapolis.

COMMISSIONERS OF ANNAPOLIS IN 1694.

Major JOHN HAMMOND,
Major EDWARD DORSEY,
Mr. JOHN BENNETT,
Mr. JOHN DORSEY,
Mr. ANDREW NORWOOD,
Mr. PHILIP HOWARD,
Mr. JAMES SANDERS,
Hon. NICHOLAS GREENBERRY, Esq.

CORPORATION OF ANNAPOLIS IN 1894.

Mayor:
JOHN H. THOMAS.

City Counsellor:
ELIHU S. RILEY.

Aldermen:

First Ward—CHARLES G. FELDMEYER.
JOHN H. BRIGHT.

Second Ward—ALLEN McCULLOUGH,
LOUIS J. GARDINER.

Third Ward—CLARENCE M. JONES,
WILLIAM H. BUTLER.

OFFICERS OF THE CITY OF ANNAPOLIS, 1894.

CLERK:
THOS. HIMELHEBER.

TREASURER:
WM. H. RULLMAN.

CITY COMMISSIONER:
EDGAR HUTTON.

MARKET MASTER:
J. HICKS RUSSELL.

HEALTH OFFICER:
DR. FRANK H. THOMPSON.

MESSENGER:
JOHN H. CAULK.

CHIEF OF POLICE:
ARTHUR MARTIN.

POLICE OFFICERS:
EZEKIEL A. MITCHELL,
JAMES W. WATKINS,
R. VINTON THOMAS,
JNO. R. TYDINGS,
SAMUEL FRANTUM,
WM. T. BROOKS.

Committees of Arrangement of the Bi-Centennial Celebration, March 5, 1894.

ON THE PART OF THE LEGISLATURE.

SENATE.

THOMAS G. HAYES,
OSWALD TILGHMAN,
THOMAS PARRAN,
WASHINGTON WILKINSON,
ROBERT MOSS.

HOUSE.

THOMAS S. BAER,
HAROLD SCARBORO,
NORMAN B. SCOTT, Jr.,
GEORGE E. KEENAN,
JOHN O. PHILLIPS,
TILGHMAN J. FAHRNEY,
A. FREDERICK GEORGE,
JAMES R. BRASHEARS,
J. HEMSLEY JOHNSON.

ON THE PART OF THE CITY OF ANNAPOLIS.

JOHN H. THOMAS,
ELIHU S. RILEY,
CHARLES G. FELDMEYER.

ON THE PART OF ST. JOHN'S COLLEGE.

NICHOLAS BREWER,
J. SCHAAF STOCKETT,
MARSHALL OLIVER, AND
DR. THOMAS FELL, *Ex Officio*,
President of St. John's College.

MEETING OF CITIZENS OF ANNAPOLIS

IN THE ASSEMBLY ROOMS.

Annapolis, February 23, 1894.

At a meeting of the citizens of Annapolis, called by the committee of arrangements of the City Council, the following business was transacted: On motion of Chas. G. Feldmeyer, Dr. J. M. Worthington was nominated for chairman, but being unable to remain was excused. Mr. Frank A. Monroe was then nominated and elected. On motion of the same gentleman, Dr. George T. Feldmeyer was named and elected Secretary. At the request of Mr. A. McCullough, of the City Council of Annapolis, Mr. E. S. Riley made a statement, explaining the object of the meeting, the necessity of appointing committees, and the duties pertaining to the same, giving a general outline of the processions, and the exercises of the day. Mr. J. S. M. Basil, Jr., then moved that there be a masquerade parade between 7 and 8.30 P. M., and that during that time the citizens be requested to illuminate their homes and places of business, and that the line of procession be over the same route as that of the afternoon parade.

Mr. Riley moved that a committee of ten be appointed by the chair, which shall be the Committee on Finance. The Chair appointed as follows:

> F. A. Munroe,
> Geo. Moss,
> Jno. W. Nason,
> J. Howard Iglehart.
> S. B. Hardy,
> R. L. Werntz,
> Wm. M. Abbott,
> C. W. Martin,
> Jno. Hangartner,
> Malcolm Watson.

On motion of Mr. A. McCullough, the chair appointed following Masquerade Committee:

> J. S. M. Basil, Jr.,
> C. A. L. Wilson,
> Jas. D. Feldmeyer,
> W. F. Basil,
> Edgar Hutton,
> Addie Stites,
> C. Weiss,
> James Strange.

It was moved by Mr. Jno. Hangartner and seconded, that this organization give a ball on the evening of the celebration, March 5th, and that the proceeds go towards defraying the expenses of the ball, the balance, if any, be handed over to the Finance Committee. Carried. The Chair appointed the following Ball Committee:

> JNO. HANGARTNER,
> ERNEST BROCK,
> SAML. GATES,
> FRANK MYERS,
> C. W. MARTIN,
> ZACK MERRIKEN,
> FRANK BASIL,
> DAVID JEWELL,
> ALFRED PARKINSON,
> JAS. STRANGE.

On motion of Mr. A. McCullough, the Chief Marshal and his first assistant were ordered to wear orange and black sashes, and the assistants blue sash and white gloves.

On motion of Mr. Riley, the Chief Marshal was authorized to make all necessary arrangements, and to make any change for the improvement of the parade. The meeting then, on motion, adjourned.

DR. GEORGE T. FELDMEYER,
Secretary.

The several committees met at various times, and fully perfected all their arrangements, entering into their work with spirit and executing all the duties assigned them with skill and fidelity. The Chief Marshal, Allen McCullough, Esq., and his first assistant, Mr. Joseph M.

Basil, were most assiduous in their labors, and performed the exacting obligations of their positions with a keen appreciation of their duties and loyalty to their demands. To the Chief Marshal's patient and unsparing efforts are due much of the success of the celebration.

INVITATION.

The following was the official invitation issued by the city of Annapolis:

ANNAPOLIS, MD., February 27, 1894.

MY DEAR SIR:

You are cordially invited to be present March 5th, 1894, to witness the celebration of the Two Hundredth Anniversary of the Removal of the Capital from Saint Mary's city to Annapolis, Maryland.

The parade will start at one o'clock P. M., and the exercises will close with a ball at night.

F. A. MUNROE, President,
DR. G. T. FELDMEYER, Secretary,
Citizens' Meeting.

J. H. THOMAS, Mayor,
E. S. RILEY, Counsellor,
C. G. FELDMEYER, Alderman,
Committee of Arrangements on part of City Council.

A. McCULLOUGH,
Chief Marshal.

J. S. M. BASIL, JR.,
First Assistant Marshal.

A CARD TO CITIZENS.

Annapolis, February 20, 1894.

The undersigned, Committee of Arrangements for the celebration of the 200th Anniversary of the removal of the Capital from St. Mary's county to Annapolis, respectfully request our citizens to decorate their residences on March 5th, with the colors of the State and Nation, and to illuminate their houses on the evening of the same, between the hours of 7 and 8.30 p. m. The Committee urges all of our citizens to lend their assistance to make the celebration a notable event.

The Committee further respectfully requests all merchants and business men of every occupation to close their places of business on March 5, from 12 noon, for the rest of the day.

John H. Thomas,
Elihu S. Riley,
Charles G. Feldmeyer,
Committee of the City Council.

OFFICIAL PROGRAM.

The following was the official program of the formation of the line of procession:

FIRST DIVISION.
Marshal in Charge—G. T. Feldmeyer.
Mounted Police.
Band.
City Council.
Ex-Mayors.
Clergy.

Committee of the Maryland Legislature.
Cadets of St. John's College.
Public School Children.

First Division will report on West street, right resting opposite Suit's Store, at 1.30 P. M.

SECOND DIVISION.

Marshal in Charge—Julian Brewer.
United States Marines.
Uniform Rank Knights of Pythias.
Rescue Hose Company.
Independent Fire Company.
Water Witch H. & L. Company.

Second Division will report at the city limits, West street, at 1.30 P. M.

THIRD DIVISION.

Marshal in Charge—F. A. Munroe.
Independent Order of Odd Fellows.
Improved Order of Red Men.
Knights of Pythias.
Junior Order of American Mechanics.
General Society of Colonial Wars.
Historical Society.

Third Division will report at the Railroad Crossing, West street, at 1.30 P. M.

MARSHALS.

The Marshals of the Second and Third Divisions will keep a space of forty feet between the divisions, and also see that each organization will keep the proper position assigned them in the procession and have the line formed to move promptly at 2 P. M.

By order of

ALLEN McCULLOUGH,
Chief Marshal.

LINE OF MARCH.

The procession formed on West street extended at 1:30 o'clock, and moved down West street to Church Circle, to Duke of Gloucester street, to Green street, to Market Space, around Market Space to Main street, to Church circle, to School street, to right of State circle, to Maryland avenue, to Hanover street, to Bridge, to King George, to Randall, to Prince George, to College campus, and dismiss.

The members of the City Council, Ex-Mayors, Clergy, Committee of the Legislature and the invited guests met at the Council Chamber at 1 P. M., and the Naval Academy band reported there at the same hour.

THE DAY.

MONDAY, MARCH 5. 1894.

THE day dawned glorious for the celebration; not a cloud dimmed the sky, and the warm air made the atmosphere delightful. The early dawn brought the stir of coming events. The stores were besieged by residents for bunting for decorations, and these repositories of bunting being soon exhausted, the citizens were driven to unique devices to satisfy their patriotic desires. From harbor as well as town floated flags and streamers, and from the venerable State House waved the Star-Spangled Banner with the sable and gold of Maryland's flag. The effect was beautiful and inspiring, especially along Main street, which was one avenue of colors. The fealty to Union as well as State was evinced by the intertwining on the private residences, of the national and State colors. It was Annapolis' best and greatest of gala days. Every train brought its addition until a multitude filled the ancient capital. The bright weather, the charming decorations, the patriotic associations and the anticipation of coming pleasures made a cheerful city, which ended as it began, with most perfect order and profound good will, a harbinger of love and respect that may forever remain amongst the noble and patriotic people of Maryland.

THE STREET PARADE.

The first event of the day, and the chief spectacular one, was the afternoon parade. Over six hundred persons, mounted, in carriages and on foot, took part in this, and were more or less decorated. The procession formed on West street, beyond the Annapolis, Washington and Baltimore depot, shortly after one o'clock. It was made up of the head and three divisions, as follows:

Chief Marshal, Allen McCullough; assistants, Joseph S. M. Basil, L. J. M. Boyd, Dr. J. M. Worthington, S. B. Hardy, W. H. Rullman, Charles Duvall. All wore orange and black sashes, black clothing, derby hats and white gloves. Their saddle-blankets were white, with black borders.

First Division—Marshal, G. T. Feldmeyer; assistants, J. H. Musterman, T. Brice, J. Trautwein, C. Weiss, C. W. Martin, W. F. Basil, J. E. Abbott, J. K. Scherger, Frank Thomas, Frank Stockett, Jr., M. M. Smith, John Boessel, Edward Taylor, G. T. Melvin, Oden Duvall, A. Phillips.

A squad of mounted police, under Chief Arthur G. Martin.

The Naval Academy Band, Charles Zimmerman, leader.

The officials of the Annapolis city government in carriages — Mayor, John H. Thomas; City Counsellor, Elihu S. Riley; Aldermen, Charles G. Feldmeyer, John H. Bright; William H. Butler.

Ex-Mayors in a carriage—James H. Brown, Abram Claude, Thomas E. Martin and James Munroe.

The clergy of the city—Dr. H. H. Clarke, of the Naval Academy; Rev. W. L. McDowell, Rev. Mr. McIlvane, Rev. Watson Case, Rev. Fathers Lowekamp, Cunningham, Cook and Hanley, of Annapolis.

General societies of colonial wars, represented by Henry Stockbridge, Jr., Thomas Marsh Smith, William Harrison Gill and George Norbury Mackenzie, who rode in carriages.

Maryland Historical Society, represented by Rev. John G. Morris, Henry F. Thompson and Edwin Warfield, who rode in carriages.

Committee from the General Assembly—Messrs. Baer, Brashears and George.

United States Marines, under Captain James M. T. Young.

Battalion of Cadets from St. John's College, under Lieutenant Robert H. Noble.

A large number of Annapolis public school children, with their teachers; the boys carried a large flag, and the girls were driven in gaily-decorated wagons.

Second Division—Marshal, Julian Brewer; assistants, Raymond Moss, F. Basil, R. G. Chaney, F. Slama, J. D. Feldmeyer, G. Gladen, Z. Merriken, Harry Brewer, A. Hopkins, Edgar Hopkins, John Nason, W. H. Smith, C. Ridout, E. F. Arnold, Burly Duvall, James E. Tate.

Annapolis Drum Corps.

Uniform Rank, Knights of Pythias, under Capt. P. Elwood Porter.

Rescue Hose Company, with men and machines, under Foreman, David B. Jewell.

Independent Fire Company, with machines.

Water Witch Hook and Ladder Company, men and machines, under Foreman, E. A. Shjourdan.

Third Division—Marshal, F. A. Munroe, assistants, Harry Feldmeyer, W. H. Thomas, Guy Thompson, James Strange, Thomas Linthicum, J. B. Martin, W. H. Moss, A. Stites, C. A. L. Wilson, C. E. Meyers, J. P. Pettibone, Walter Clark, W. M. Holladay, Charles Pettibone, C. Duvall, Jr., R. W. Tate, D. R. Magruder.

Woodberry Fife and Drum Corps.

Independent Order of Odd Fellows, eight representatives from Metropolis Lodge, No. 17, as follows: J. W. Connolly, Samuel Davis, D. O. Parlett, Daniel Medford, A. L. Baker, Lee Kalmey, Wm. Gibbs and Wm. Redmond. They were in regalia and rode in carriages.

Improved Order of Red Men in two hacks, twelve mounted and about thirty on foot. Those in carriages and mounted were in regalia. The mounted men wore painted masks. The former were Prof. A. J. Corbesier, R. V. Clayton, Lewis H. Rhen, W. Henry Burtis, Percy Parlett, Brewer Gardner, Wm. V. Morris and Robert W. Clayton, Jr.

Knights of Pythias, under Chancellor Commander Weems Ridout.

Junior Order of American Mechanics, forty in number, under Captain Frank Shaw.

The procession moved down West street to Church Circle, to Duke of Gloucester street, to Green street, to Market Space, around Market Space to Main street, to Church Circle, to School street, to right of State Circle, to Maryland avenue, to Hanover street, to Bridge, to King George, to Randall, to Prince George, to College campus, and there dismissed.

Crowds viewed the parade from every point along the route and cheered the various divisions. An unusually large crowd assembled about the St. John's College campus to witness the disbanding.

MASQUERADE, ILLUMINATION AND BALL.

The masquerade, between seven and eight-thirty o'clock P. M., proved a most successful part of the day's program. Several hundred took part in the parade; many of the characters were marked caricatures, and the complete procession a splendid conclusion to the pageants of the day. The enjoyment of the spectacle was largely interfered with by an accident at the electric light works that cut off the arc lamps and put the streets in darkness.

The illumination of the residences of citizens, during the hours of the masquerade, mitigated in some degree the loss of the street lamps, and gave cheerful color to the merry proceedings in the city.

The ball, at the Masonic Assembly Rooms, was an enjoyable ending to the day's proceedings. There was a fairly, but not excessively, large attendance.

ON THE PART OF ST. JOHN'S COLLEGE.

The faculty of St. John's, the Board of Governors and Visitors, and alumni of the College, at the conclusion of the afternoon's parade, were escorted from McDowell Hall to the Masonic Opera House, where the following exercises were observed:

Scripture Reading, Psalm I, and Prayer, by Rev. H. H. Clarke, D. D., Chaplain U. S. Navy.

Song—"My Maryland,"—The Children of the Public Schools of Annapolis, Md.

Address—"An Early Sample of Free Religion and Free Education,"—Adjutant-General H. Kyd Douglas, of Hagerstown, Md.

Song—"Star-Spangled Banner."—The Children of the Public School of Annapolis, Md.

Address—"The Capital of St. Mary's,"—J. W. Thomas, Esq., of Cumberland, Md.

Song—"Hail Columbia."—The Children of the Public School of Annapolis, Md.

Announcements—By the President, Thomas Fell, of St. John's College.

Dr. Fell said that the Board of Governors and Visitors of St. John's College had arrived at the conclusion that they could only confer degrees at commencement day. The Board, therefore, wishing to honor some of its friends and alumni, directed him to say that (D. V.,) the Board would confer at its next commencement day, June 28th, the following degrees:

Honorary degree of doctor of laws:

Hon. John M. Robinson, graduated from Dickinson College; Chief Judge of the Court of Appeals, Maryland.

Hon. Henry D. Harlan, graduated from St. John's College, B. A., '78; M. A., '87; Chief Judge of the Supreme Bench of Baltimore city.

Hon. James Revell, graduated from St. John's College, B. A. '49; M. A. '53; member of the Board of Visitors and Governors; Associate Judge of the Fifth Judicial Circuit of Maryland.

Hon. Somerville P. Tuck; graduated from the University of Virginia, B. A., '67; St. John's College, M. A., '88; recently appointed Judge of the International Court of Alexandria, Egypt.

Honorary Degree of Doctor of Divinity— Rev. Edward C. Macnichol, of Pocomoke City, Md., graduated from Dickinson Theological Seminary, '74; member of the Wilmington Conference of the Methodist Episcopal Church.

Benediction by Rev. Adolphus Pindell, an alumnus of St. John's College.

Literary and Religious Ceremonies

ON THE PARTS OF THE

City of Annapolis and State of Maryland,

IN THE

HALL OF THE HOUSE OF DELEGATES,

MONDAY, MARCH 5, 1894.

At 8:30 P. M.

PROGRAMME.

Prayer by Rev. W. S. Southgate, D. D., Rector of St. Anne's Protestant Episcopal Church, Annapolis.

1. "Hail Columbia Happy Land."
2. Opening remarks by Thomas S. Baer, Member of Committee on part of House of Delegates.
3. "Yankee Doodle."
4. Essay, "The Removal of the Capital from St. Mary's to Annapolis," by Elihu S. Riley, of Annapolis, Md.
5. "Maryland, My Maryland," words paraphrased to a hymn on our Public Schools.
6. Address, "The Catholic and Puritan Settlements in Maryland," by Prof. Alfred P. Dennis, of Princeton, New Jersey.
7. "My Native Country, Thee."

Benediction by Rev. Father Lowekamp, Rector of St. Mary's Catholic Church, Annapolis.

"Star Spangled Banner," as the audience dispersed. The Singing was by a Chorus from the Public Schools of Annapolis.

Ushers—MESSRS. FENTON LEE DUVALL,
PETER H. MAGRUDER,
E. BERKELY IGLEHART,
JOHN R. MAGRUDER,
T. KENT GREEN.

Amongst the audience were: Captain R. L. Phythean, Superintendent of Naval Academy; Lieutenant Commander Uriel Sebree, U. S. N.; Lieutenant Commander B. F. Tilley, U. S. N.; Lieutenant Commander Asa Walker, U. S. N.; Lieutenant Commander J. E. Craig, U. S. N.; Lieutenant Commander G. P. Colvocorresses, U. S. N., in full uniform; invited guests of the committee on the part of the city of Annapolis.

Gov. Brown was also in attendance.

The following teachers of the Girls' Public School were present to assist the pupils in singing: Miss Elizabeth Dorsey, principal, Miss Milicent Redmond, Miss R. G. Camden, Miss Elenora W. Pindell, Miss Anna S. Brady, Miss Josephine Reardon, Miss Cora Medley, Miss Bessie Tate.

1694.

KING WILLIAM'S SCHOOL,

For which the initiatory steps were taken in 1694, was the progenitor of St. John's College.

The earliest Board of Trustees of King William's School to be found in the records, is that of 1696, the laws of 1694, as a whole, having been lost, and the Board of Trustees with it.

The Board of Trustees of 1696 was:

FRANCIS NICHOLSON, ESQ., GOVERNOR,
HON. SIR THOMAS LAWRENCE, BARONET,
COL. GEORGE ROBOTHAM,
COL. CHARLES HUTCHINS,
COL. JOHN ADDISON,
    OF THE GOVERNOR'S COUNCIL.

REV. PEREGRINE CONY,
REV. JOHN HEWETT,
ROBERT SMITH,
KENELM CHELSELDYNE,
HENRY COURSEY,
EDWARD DORSEY,

THOMAS ENNALS,
THOMAS TASKER,
FRANCIS JENKINS,
WILLIAM DENT,
THOMAS SMITH,
EDWARD BOOTHBY,
JOHN THOMPSON,
JOHN BIGGER,
        Gentlemen.

1894.

Board of Visitors and Governors Of St. John's College.

PRESIDENT:
(*Ex-Officio.*)
His Excellency, FRANK BROWN,
The Governor of Maryland,
Annapolis, Md., 1892.

(*Under the Charter elected annually,*)
FRANK H. STOCKETT,*
Annapolis, Md., 1848.

SECRETARY:
Hon. NICHOLAS BREWER,*
Annapolis, Md., 1857.

EX-OFFICIO.

Hon. JOHN W. SMITH, President of the Senate,
                              Snow Hill, Md.

Hon. JAMES H. PRESTON, Speaker of the House of Delegates,
                              Baltimore, Md.

Hon. J. M. ROBINSON, Chief Judge Court of Appeals,
                              Centreville, Md.

Hon. W. SHEPARD BRYAN, Judge Court of Appeals,
                              Baltimore, Md.

Hon. DAVID FOWLER, Judge Court of Appeals,
                              Towson, Md.

Hon. JAMES McSHERRY, Judge Court of Appeals,
                              Frederick, Md.

Hon. JOHN P. BRISCOE, Judge Court of Appeals,
                              Prince Frederick, Md.

*Graduated from St. John's.

HON. HENRY PAGE, Judge Court of Appeals,
                                    Princess Anne, Md.
HON. CHARLES B. ROBERTS, Judge Court of Appeals,
                                    Westminster, Md.
HON. A. HUNTER BOYD, Judge Court of Appeals,
                                    Cumberland, Md.

ELECTIVE BY THE BOARD OF GOVERNORS AND VISITORS.

JAMES MACKUBIN, Ellicott City, Md., 1852.
HON. DANIEL M. HENRY, Cambridge, Md., 1857.
DANIEL M. THOMAS, Baltimore, Md., 1859.
SPRIGG HARWOOD, Annapolis, Md., 1861.
JAMES MUNROE, Annapolis, Md., 1869.
WILLIAM HARWOOD, Annapolis, Md., 1873.
J. SHAAFF STOCKETT, Annapolis, Md., 1878.
WILLIAM R. HAYWARD, M. D., Cambridge, Md., 1878.
GEORGE WELLS, M. D., Annapolis, Md., 1882.
HON. JOHN S. WIRT, Elkton, Md., 1882.
WILLIAM G. RIDOUT, M. D., Annapolis, Md., 1882.
HON. J. WIRT RANDALL, Annapolis, Md., 1882.
RICHARD M. VENABLE, Baltimore, Md., 1884.
RICHARD H. GREEN, Annapolis, Md., 1884.
PHILEMON H. TUCK, Baltimore, Md., 1885.
RICHARD M. CHASE, Annapolis, Md., 1887.
MARSHAL OLIVER, U. S. N., Annapolis, Md., 1891.
L. DORSEY GASSAWAY, Annapolis, Md., 1891.
SPENCER C. JONES, Annapolis, Md., 1891.
DANIEL R. MAGRUDER, Annapolis, Md., 1892.
BLANCHARD RANDALL, Baltimore, Md., 1892.
JAMES REVELL, Annapolis, Md., 1893.

These figures refer to the date of the election of the several members of the Boards.

THE FACULTY.

THOMAS FELL, A. M., Ph. D., LL. D., President, Professor of Moral Science and Ancient Languages.

JAMES W. CAIN, A. M., (Graduate of Yale College,) Professor of Political and Social Science.

JOHN L. CHEW, A. M., (Graduate of St. John's College,) Professor of Mathematics.

ROBERT H. NOBLE, LL. B., First Lieut. U. S. Army, (Graduate of University of Maryland,) Professor of Military Science and Tactics, and Lecturer on International and Constitutional Law.

JOHN D. EPES, B. A., (Graduate of Randolph-Macon College,) Professor of English and English Literature.

HENRI MARION, Professor of Modern Languages.

GEORGE RIPLEY PINKHAM, A. M., (Graduate of Brown University,) Professor of Greek.

W. M. BERKELEY, B. A., (Graduate of University of Virginia,) Professor of Natural Sciences.

JOSEPH R. WILMER, B. A., U. S. N., (Graduate of St. John's College and U. S. Naval Academy,) Professor of Physics and Mechanical Engineering.

EDWIN D. PUSEY, A. M., (Graduate of St. John's College,) Assistant Professor of Latin and German.

Rev. W. S. T. DEAVOR, Ph. D., (Graduate of Allegany College,) Assistant Professor of Mathematics.

FRANCIS E. DANIELS, A. M., (Graduate of St. John's College), Assistant Professor of Botany and Biology.

FRED. WILLING, A. M., (Graduate of Hobart College), Special Instructor in Charge of Candidates for the U. S. Naval Academy.

JAMES P. BIAYS, Jr., B. A., Instructor in Preparatory School.

KARL KUHL, Secretary for the President,

PRAYER

OFFERED BY

REV. H. H. CLARKE, D. D.,

CHAPLAIN U. S. N.,

At the exercises on behalf of St. John's College, at the Masonic Opera House, on March 5, 1894, in honor of the Bi-Centennial Celebration of the initiatory movement to found King William's School, the progenitor of St. John's College.

We thank thee, our Heavenly Father, that thou art the God of the world; that thou art the Lord of the centuries, even as of the years. As we look into fragments, detachments of time, we can see thy plan, as we also behold it, running through long periods of continuous history. Thy purpose of right-doing toward mankind gathers to itself increasing light, whether followed as it moves along the course of years or of centuries. Thou dost reign in justice and kindness, regarding the happiness of thy creatures, more than even the showing forth of thy glory. We praise thee for what thou hast done for this land of ours. In the beginning thou didst send the right men to it; those who loved the truth; those who were willing to suffer and die for it. They came with a deep love for what had been made known by consciences enlightened, by a sense of justice deepened, by a hope of human welfare and progress strengthened. Under thy guidance they did their work. They gave to us our original Commonwealths; planted the seeds of everything great and good in our whole loved land. We thank thee for the part taken by the Colony and the State of Maryland for the good of the whole people; that upon this soil were given such early and inspiring lessons of religious and political freedom. We praise thee for what education here accomplished for these ends; that this institution was early planted on the shores of the Chesapeake to be a source of enlightenment and an instrument of good, ministering to what the State is now so justly proud of. May it be blessed more and more, widening in usefulness and influence in accordance with its venerable character and high purpose. Continue thy blessing upon its living graduates; help its president and its faculty in all their work; let thy love and care be extended to each of its students; so let it prosper in the present and in the future. Upon all the exercises of this occasion may thy blessing descend. All of which we offer and ask, for Christ's sake, amen.

AN ADDRESS

DELIVERED BY

ADJUTANT-GEN'L H. KYD DOUGLAS,

By invitation of the Board of Governors and Visitors of St. John's College, at the Masonic Opera House, March 5, 1894, at the ceremonies that day on behalf of the College, on the Bi-Centennial Celebration of the initiation of King William's School, the progenitor of St. John's College.

An Early Sample of Free Religion and Free Education.

For ten or more years we have had an epidemic of centennials. Few events, over fifty years of age, have escaped it. We have had centennials and semi-centennials, bi-centennials and tri-centennials; and our recent quadro-centennial was one of the wonders of the age—the admiration alike of Christendom and Heathendom. All this was very natural. Nations are very like individuals because they are made up of individuals, and when they pass adolescence, they take great pride in their maturity and are anxious to celebrate it and have a good time. The Americans, too, may be relied upon to try to do everything better and oftener than any other people, and the States of the Union vie with each other in getting up sensational effects.

Maryland, as is her wont, has kept up with the procession, and to-day, as something of a variety, is combining two or three such entertainments—a bi-centennial of the removal of the State Capital from St. Mary's to Annapolis—the bi-centennial of the foundation of King William's School, with a brief repetition of the centennial of St. John's College as the only heir at law and residuary legatee of King William's. This is very well. Maryland has never made enough of her past. Whatever may be said of other States, she certainly has never claimed the earth. In fact, she might have taken some valuable hints from other sister Commonwealths, notably those founded by her early Puritan rivals, where skillful and partisan historians have well imitated the French cook who can make soup enough for twenty people out of the hind leg of a frog. Take any small event in the history of one of those States and you will find half a dozen local historians who will tell you all about it, with no end of apocryphal addenda. And then they have such inimitable adroitness in skating swiftly over discreditable places, with graceful gestures to divert attention and conceal the thinnesss of the ice and the muddy water beneath!

Whether it is better to be cleverly unscrupulous or stupidly indifferent to the record of one's State, I will leave to experts in moral polemics. The sins of the literary sons of Maryland have been those of omission. She has had scholarly and eloquent men of leisure and fortune, whose brilliancy and learning were of the highest standard, and yet with abundance of material at hand, they seem to have lacked either the pride, or patriotism, or industry, to do what they might have done to place our State in its proper position upon the shelves of interesting historical literature. Many valuable historic facts have been hidden by rubbish and forgotten; they should be brought forth and given to our people and the people of other States in logical arrangement and attractive form. It is not too late. The history of Maryland is brilliant with glories in forum and field — splendid examples in the records of Church and State. Perhaps there is some one in this audience who will catch the inspiration from this day's proceedings and hereafter build his own monument in the history of his native State.

In 1633, two little vessels, of blessed memory, the Ark and the Dove, brought from England into the Chesapeake Bay that small colony of two hundred adventurous souls who settled the province of Maryland. From the first they began to build well. The first oath taken by the chief Governor of the Province in 1648, contained a sentence which has been transmitted to us in our Bill of Rights—

4

"I will not, for fear, favor, affection, or any other cause, let, hinder or delay justice to any."

What could have induced these same wise and far-seeing statesmen, not much later to have taken such violent and unreasonable prejudice against lawyers as to have declared them "one of the grand grievances of the colony," and to have passed a law in 1674, "to reform attorneys, councillors, &c.," I can not imagine; indeed, I can not see how in the world, a reformed lawyer, or even a regular, kept from starvation, practicing law in the woods among a few hundred scurvy impecunious refugees—I mean peaceful, impoverished law abiding patriots! But lawyers, like prophets and apostles and doctors, and many other christian gentlemen, have had a hard time of it in all ages; and only by the most unremitting industry and devotion to duty and ducats have they been able to take care of themselves.

As early as 1649, a law was passed in Maryland that "no one within this province professing to believe in Jesus Christ shall be any way, troubled, molested or discountenanced for his or her religion or in the free exercise thereof." Speaking of the early settlement of this Colony, Bancroft has said without exaggeration—"its history is the history of benevolence, gratitude and toleration," and he elsewhere says, "here religious liberty obtained a home, its only home in the wide world. Every other country had persecuting laws, till through the benign administration of the Government of Maryland, no person professing to believe in Jesus Christ was permitted to be molested on account of religion." The same celebrated historian places Lord Baltimore among the wisest and most benevolent lawgivers of all ages.

New England was colonized by Puritans fleeing from persecution, Maryland by Catholics seeking religious freedom, Virginia by Episcopalians of the Church of England. When the record of each is brought to light in this tolerant age, Maryland alone need not be ashamed. The Episcopalians of Virginia enacted severe legislation for the suppression of Presbyterians, Friends, Puritans and other dissenters, in order to force them out of the colony. The harsher and more cruel measures of New England Puritans, with whom exile, scourging, burning, torture and death were common punishments, are familiar to the readers of American history.

But it is the pride of Maryland (and if you have heard it often it will not harm you to hear it again), that upon her early history there is no such dark stain. At times sporadic cases of intolerance—the germs brought from England in their old clothes—seemed to threaten serious disease, but the air of Maryland soon proved a religious disinfectant. Thanks to the benign example of Lord

Baltimore, with that broad Catholicism which has distinguished the history of the State, the breath of prayer on this colony soon became as free as the air of her mountains and as pure as the streams of her valleys. Since then religious freedom, the veritable vine and fig tree longed for since the olden time, has flourished everywhere on this broad continent. From Maryland, over America—from America, over the civilized world, has spread this doctrine of creed and constitution that there can be no liberty without religious liberty. Religion has nothing to fear from liberty and reason; and it is worthy of note and comment, that those States of the Union, in which, when provinces, there were the greatest intolerance and fanaticism, are now the camping grounds of scepticism and unbelief. The world has learned, at last, that violence can not kill infidelity nor make faith universal.

It was thus that Maryland was baptized in love and gratitude as "The Land of the Sanctuary." Higher than titles of rank and badges of honor, more significant than heraldic motto, more noble than the nobility of royalty, more to be venerated than the sacred memory which consecrates the history of that old State house, greatest of all her trophies and glories, is the simple and graceful title which her faith and toleration won for our good old State, "The Land of the Sanctuary."

As you have been told, and will be told again before to-day is over, the seat of government of the Maryland province was in 1694 moved from St. Mary's to Anne Arundel town, which soon after received the more euphonious name of Annapolis. The population of Maryland then was about 25,000.

One of the first acts of the General Assembly of the year 1694, was the passage of an act *"for the advancement of learning,"* by which there was to be a school, some day to ripen into a college and then to expand into a University, "for the education of the youth of the Province in *good letters and manners.*" The earnest founders of the colony believed in the inspired truth of that one of the Proverbs, (8:11.) "For wisdom is better than rubies; and all things that may be desired are not to be compared to it." The project was beautiful and commendable, and we can well fancy the wise looks upon the solemn faces of these early law-makers as they stroked their beards and voted "aye" for these wise and pregnant bills. It is true that from the high literary standpoint of this age and this audience, it may be thought that the members of that august body slightly gave themselves away when they defined the institution they were then organizing as "a *free school* for Latin, Greek, *writing and the like.*" But when we pause and linger over the words, and get at the purpose of those early laws, our amusement changes to admiration; and when we strike that little sentence, "a free school," we recall with State pride, the pleasing fact that by the act of that Legislature, there was solemnly and wisely organized and established the first free school in Maryland, the first free school in America! There was to be no limit to its benefits, no patrician pupilage, no sectarian restrictions; but the advancement of learning, good letters and manners was to be free to all the little colony of Maryland, and within her borders and for all her people, free religion and free education were to go hand in hand. What State can point to such a combination so early in its history?

The institution thus established was, by subsequent legislation in 1696, called King William's School, in honor of the King then reigning in England, and may be considered as a younger brother of William and Mary's College then established in Virginia, but with more liberal ideas as to the freedom of education than her more aristocratic neighbor.

The new schoolhouse for King William's School was built, it seems, principally from donations of tobacco, at that time the chief currency of the province. I can sympathize with the sad condition of the colonists, who in the absence of free silver were driven to such straits, but I am obstinate in the belief that if those plain old patriots had foreseen the day when the advancement of learning and good manners in 1894 would fill the atmosphere of college halls, libraries and parlors with the smoke and scent of the omnipresent and malodorous cigarette, they would have thrown down their old pipes in prophetic dismay, have left the college unendowed and the schoolhouse unbuilt! What they would have thought of base ball and foot ball as academic promoters of education and civilization, my feeble imagination fails to suggest!

For the further support of free schools the General Assembly laid an imposition on the exportation of beef, bacon, bear skins, otter, wildcat, fox and wolf skins, muskrats, raccoons and many other articles of sport and profit; a kind of primitive reverse tariff which if added to the price of the article, was a sure way of making the foreigner pay the tax. They also had a kind of tariff on importations for the same purpose, but, as there were no "infant industries" then, it was purely a tariff for revenue. At any rate our forbears were determined to have free schools, and they knew how to raise the money to support them; nor did they have any dead locks, filibusterings and bad blood over the way in which it was done.

King William's School, thus founded with prayerful endeavors and high hopes, continued its work with more or less success until the outbreak of the Revolution. Then Latin, Greek and good manners went to the rear as teachers and students were called to the front, and, instead of studying history, began to make it. For the time the schoolhouse was deserted, and the advancement of learning collapsed. After the Revolution was over, it revived in a feeble and bloodless sort of way, but, as King William's School, it never again got successfully to work.

In 1784, the General Assembly of Maryland incorporated and founded St. John's College at Annapolis, and the following year legislated all the property, funds, masters and scholars of King William's School into it. We all know after whom King Willam's School was named, but whether St. John's owes its beautiful name to St. John the Baptist, or St. John the evangelist, I find no record, and must leave the question to be solved by theological antiquarians. From the bountiful supply of water in the vicinity, I am disposed to think that some of the special followers of the Baptist had a hand in that patronymic legislation and wanted future scholars to be kept clean in flesh as well as in faith. I do not, however, insist upon this suggestion, for I remember that among the first promoters and patrons of St. John's College were the Catholic Bishop of Baltimore, the Episcopal Bishop of Maryland, the highest Presbyterian clergyman in the State, and so far as I know, there was not a Baptist preacher in the Commonwealth. Be that as it may, it was a fair omen of the College to have it begin its career under the auspices of so much sectarian liberality, and, if it has not flourished, as it should have done, it was not for the want of ample blessings at the start. It should have been considered another good omen, that on the day the College was first formally opened, on the 11th of November, 1789, Francis Scott Key was enrolled as a student "for instruction in learning and virtue." He afterwards wrote his name on our flag, and there it will remain forever. Not a hundred years old, modern patriots may call it "Old Glory," but it has been baptized in all history, song and story as the "Star-Spangled Banner." Following him comes a long list of men, eminent in State and Nation, prominent in art, science, literature and all the professions, who, as alumni of St. John's College, have lived and died in affectionate regard for her as their alma mater.

I am impressed with the conviction that it was unfortunate and most injurious that St. John's College was from the beginning so closely connected with the State House and State Government. Very early its Governors and Boards of Visitors learned, too easily, to put their trust in princes and to look to the State House for aid and encouragement. This proved to be delusive and unwise. There are other things legislatures take more interest in than the advancement of learning, and the average local statesman is apt to meet the appeal of the professor in the spirit of that distinguished practical politician of Pennsylvania, whose denunciation of those "damned literary fellows" excited the wide-spread sympathy of the craft!

Originally St. John's College had fair promises from the State. An early legislature by solemn contract endowed her with an annuity of $8,750, to be paid "annually and forever." At that time it was a goodly sum of money and created high hopes and unreasonable expectations. Soon after and just when the money was most needed, a subsequent legislature, in violation of a plain principle of constitutional law, broke this contract between the State and the College and repealed the annuity. The Court of Appeals denounced the technical violation of the Constitution, but refused the College an effective remedy. Since then the College has been almost annually standing at the doors of the legislature, sometimes receiving fair and liberal treatment, but often little aid and scant courtesy. The situation led at times to questionable expedients, among others to the Act of 1821, by which the College was authorized to raise $20,000 for its uses by a lottery. Such a scheme was a moral blight upon the College, for gambling can hardly be considered a creditable and effective instrument for the "advancement of learning and virtue."

It may be that, at first, with a scanty population and very limited means, State aid was necessary to give the institution a start in life. But in more recent years the people of the State should have taken hold of its fortunes as a matter of State pride. Colleges and universities are everywhere, rich and full of students. Men have given of their wealth to them, have founded and established them. How few of them have either history or age or any claim upon patriotic pride. Public spirit, individual enterprise and private aid have made them a success. Men with a genius for business have taken them in hand, have enlisted individual donations, demanded the attention of the public, and by industry and enthusiasm have pushed them to fortune. Why was this not done right here? What college seat has more patriotic associations than this ancient city of Annapolis? Where could a better situation be found for a University than on this Chesapeake Bay? What people in all these States gave such early evidence of their devotion to the cause of education as those of the province of Maryland? Here in this Commonwealth, where before the foundation of yonder high-domed capitol was laid, free religion was proclaimed for all her people; here in this town, where, in King William's Free School, free education was conceived and born and transmitted with lofty hopes and aspirations to the College of St. John's, before our patriotic fathers ever dreamed of that coming republic, where free religion and free education would be the inheritance of 70,000,000 of people; here in this State and in this city should live and flourish a great institution of learning worthy of the State, worthy of its history and worthy of the traditions of its people; a great university with inviting doors, swinging wide to the youth of all the land, and a store-house of that virtuous learning which fathers and mothers are seeking for their sons!

Why cannot this be!

I am not a graduate of St. John's nor a Marylander by birth, but I know something of the history of this State, and I would like to see a college on these grounds that would represent and realize her early aspirations in the cause of education. I would like to see its campus full of students, its library full of books, its management full of hope. I would like to see those wide swinging doors I speak of, and read from one this inscription, done in letters of silver: "Within these walls still lives the spirit of our good fathers, who, two centuries ago, laid the first foundation of free education on this continent, and with the torch of knowledge lighted the way to American freedom and independence;" and, on the other, this in letters of gold: "More than two hundred years ago, the new people of this colony who had given to the world and mankind the first edict for free religion, founded this school that she might preserve for all time the sacred record, and scatter through all the lands by her pupils this sacred truth, that through the early blessings of prayer and education, Maryland was called 'The Land of the Sanctuary.'"

Historical Address on St. Mary's City,

The First Capital of Maryland, delivered at Annapolis, Md., March 5, 1894, by

MR. JAMES W. THOMAS,

On the Occasion of the Celebration of the Two Hundredth Anniversary of the Removal of the Capital from St. Mary's to Annapolis, by invitation of the City of Annapolis and St. John's College.

As the place of first permanent settlement of the Maryland colony; as the seat of Maryland's first provincial capital; as the theatre of our infant struggles; and as the cradle of our civil and our religious liberty, the history of St. Mary's city is invested with peculiar interest and special inspiration; and, even though but briefly outlined, possesses singular appropriateness as a part of these ceremonies.

St. Mary's city, the first capital of Maryland, was situated on the east side of the St. Mary's river, a tributary of the Potomac, about five miles from its mouth, and sixteen miles from Point Lookout, the southern extremity of the western shore of Maryland.

A gentle slope from the eastern hills, then a spacious plateau of singular beauty, elevated about fifty feet above the water, and terminating in a bold bluff between two broad expanses of the river, formed the site of the city.

A crescent-shaped indentation, made by this bluff and a long headland about a mile lower down the river, gave the city a capacious harbor.

The river skirted two sides of the town, afforded depth and security of navigation, and adding beauty and grandeur to its other attractions, made the situation of St. Mary's one of surpassing loveliness.

A river, possessing more enchanting scenery than the St. Mary's, may not easily be found, and, at no point along its banks, is this displayed to greater advantage than at the site of old St. Mary's.

This ancient city occupied the site of the Indian village of "Yaocomico," at which place the Maryland colony was induced to settle by the glowing description of Captain Henry Fleet, son of a member of the Virginia company, whose familiarity with the country gave his opinion importance and weight, and who described it as a location desirable alike, for its commanding commercial advantages and its safety of defense, as well for its temporary improvements and its natural beauty and attractiveness, or in his own language, "a spot indeed so charming in its situation that Europe itself can scarcely show one to surpass it." An inspection of the place convinced the colony of its superior fitness, and that an entry there could be easily and safely made, owing to the fact that the Yaocomicos, to avoid the Susquehanocks, a more powerful tribe, and their enemy, were then preparing to abdicate and move higher up the country.

The colony, to avoid "every appearance of injustice and afford no opportunity for hostility" on the part of the Indians, waived all questions of right or superior power in the premises, and bought their town and territory, giving in exchange commodities, useful in their kind and satisfactory to the natives.

Much historical encomium has been lavished upon William Penn for his famous treaty with the Shackamaxon Indians for the land on which the city of Philadelphia stands, but it should here be said, that neither the annals of Pennsylvania, or of any other American colony, present a more conspicuous example of humanity and justice toward the aborigines, than is portrayed in the spirit which animated Maryland on that occasion, and indeed throughout in that regard, and it should, with equal justice, adorn the pages of its history.

The landing having been made with as much formality as circumstances would permit, Governor Calvert, on the 27th of March, 1634, with appropriate ceremonies, proclaimed formal possession of Maryland, and named its first town St. Mary's.

"Then and thus," it has been well said, "landed the pilgrims of Maryland, and then and thus were laid the foundations of the old city of St. Mary's and of our present State. The landing of the pilgrims of New England has been the burden of many a story and the theme of many an oration. The very rock upon which their feet were first planted is consecrated in the estimation of their descendants, and its relics are enshrined as objects of holy regard. They were freemen in search of freedom; they found it and transmitted it to their posterity. It becomes us therefore to tread lightly upon their ashes. Yet, while we would avoid all invidious contrasts and forget the stern spirit of the Puritan, which so often mistook religious intolerance for holy zeal, we can turn with exaltation to the pilgrims of Maryland as the founders of religious liberty in the new world. They erected the first altar to it on this continent; and the fires first kindled on it ascended to Heaven amid the blessings of the savage."

The earliest instructions from Lord Baltimore with reference to the first Maryland town, were that its locacation should be selected with due regard to "health and fruitfulness" and to facilities for "fortification" and "convenience for trade." The town located, it was to be laid out into "lots," with convenient "streets" and lanes on which the buildings were to be erected "in line" "near adjoining one to another," and to be built in as "decent and uniform a manner" as circumstances would permit; the land in the rear of the houses "to be assigned for gardens and such uses;" the first choice of lots to be for a "fit place and a competent quantity of ground for a fort," and near it. a site for a "convenient house and a church or chapel adjacent," for the "seat of his Lordship or his Governor."

Undisturbed for several years either by domestic factions or external dissensions, St. Mary's, for a colonial town, grew with considerable rapidity. Brick and other builders' supplies were imported, which, with the home products available for the purpose, afforded, from an early period, abundant building material.

While Virginia, it is said, as late as 1638, was making its laws in an ale house, and indeed, in 1716, its capital contained only "a church, court house and four other buildings," St. Mary's, in a comparatively short time after its settlement, had, besides the home of Lord Baltimore, a church, a pretentious State House, a jail and other public offices, and about thirty houses. Soon thereafter, it had sixty houses, protected by two forts, St. Mary's and St. Inigoes, each well mounted with the ordnance of that day.

As the place for holding the General Assemblies, the seat of the Provincial Court, and the port where all ships trading with the Province had first to resort, St. Mary's soon became a place of importance, and, in 1668, it was by letters patent, incorporated and erected into a city, with privileges and immunities above and beyond any other place in the Province. Its officers consisted of a mayor, recorder, six aldermen and ten councilmen, and among its special prerogatives, were those of a "weekly market" and an "annual fair," to the latter of which the ancient "Court of Pipoudre" was an incident.

In 1671, St. Mary's received a new accession to its privileges, that of sending two representatives to the General Assembly, of whom the first were Robert Carvill, subsequently Attorney-General, and Thomas Notley, afterwards Governor of Maryland.

It is to be regretted that no map or plan of St. Mary's was ever made, or, at least, is not extant. The old city, except in name and in memory, has long since passed away, and there is apparently no data from which a complete drawing can, at this day, be made.

From original surveys and grants, however, and ancient boundaries and land-marks, still visible, the general outlines of the city, and the location of its principal public and more prominent private buildings, are still susceptible of accurate identification.

The plain, upon which St. Mary's stood, was about a mile square, the limit prescribed by its charter, with a water front made extensive by the many and acute meanderings of the river. Upon this plateau the houses, which passed through the "various stages of architectural transition" from the log cabin to the substantial frame and brick building, were scattered irregularly, the lots being unsymmetrically arranged, of irregular size and large, none of them being less than a quarter of an acre, and many of them large enough for extensive grounds and gardens sufficiently capacious to supply the needs of the household.

A description of the location and architecture, even of the principal buildings at St. Mary's, would not be within the scope of this address. It may, however, be proper to say, that the improvement consisted of its fort or palissado, which, though a rude structure when compared with those of more modern date, was solidly built and well enough mounted to protect the inhabitants against the warfare of that day; its massive and dignified State House, with its thick walls, tile roof and paved floors; its stout jail, with its iron-barred windows; its market-house, warehouses and several ordinaries; its unique brick chapel, the victim of the anti-Catholic persecution of later times; its quaint Protestant church; its pretentious and fortress-like executive mansion, which, with its offices, private houses and shops, of varied architectural design, numbering, it is said, about sixty, and scattered over the elevated, but level, plain, studded, we are told, with primeval forest trees, constituted the picturesque little metropolis of early Maryland.

The first General Assembly held in Maryland met at St. Mary's on the 26th of February, 1635. The acts of this session Baltimore refused to approve, because, as he claimed, the right to originate laws resided under the charter exclusively in himself, the power of the Assembly being limited to assent and dissent to such as he propounded. The freemen of Maryland, convinced that they possessed equal and co-ordinate rights in matters of legislation, with the Proprietary, with the courage of their conviction, vindicated their position, by rejecting at the next session of the Assembly, the whole body of bills drafted and submitted by him for their adoption, and enacted in their stead, a code which emanated from themselves, though substantially the same as the one that he had propounded.

After this the right of the Assembly to initiate legislation was not contested, and the right of the Proprietary was, in practice, limited to his veto.

It should here be said that the legislation enacted at this and the succeeding sessions of the Assembly, during the sixty-one years in which St. Mary's was the seat of government, forms, to a great extent, the foundation and outlines of the present legal, civil and social structure of Maryland, and of some of its most cherished institutions.

It was then and there that the great struggle for popular sovereignty, between the bold and courageous yeomanry of Maryland and the Lord Proprietary, was inaugurated, and which resulted in setting upon a firm foundation that principle which formed the basis of Maryland's early system of free self-government, and which, "in process of time and in course of events," developed into a reality the sublime doctrine of constitutional liberty.

It was also by the legislation then and there enacted, that the famous "Toleration Act," giving legal sanction to liberty of conscience, which shed such brilliant renown upon the legislative annals of Maryland, which won for it the name of the "Land of the Sanctuary," and which extended to all, whatever their religious belief or form of worship, "shelter, protection and repose," became engrafted by law upon its government.

Though religious toleration had existed in practice in Maryland from its earliest settlement, it had never been made the subject of legislative enactment, and to the General Assembly of 1649, does this, "the proudest memorial" of Maryland's colonial history, belong.

"Higher than all titles and badges of honor," and more exalted than royal nobility, is the imperishable distinction which the passage of this broad and liberal act won for Maryland, and for the members of that never-to be-forgotten session, and sacred *forever be the hallowed spot which gave it birth!*

But, besides being the historic battle-field of Maryland's early struggles for political freedom, and the scene of its first legislative confirmation of religious peace, St. Mary's presents in its history, as the capital and metropolis of the province, all the "glowing incidents and martial virtues" which characterized and gave inspiration to that eventful and heroic period—the period in Maryland's history which has truly been styled "the golden age of its colonial existence;" the period in which the foundations of its government were being broadly and deeply laid; the period of its great political turmoils, and religious agitations; the period in which the defiant spirit and persistent rebellion of Clayborne; the artful sedition and destructive warfare of Ingle; the reflex action upon Maryland of England's parliamentary disturbances, resulting in the usurpation of the Proprietary rights; the turbulence and the ascendancy of the Puritan, whose reign was so conspicuous for its political proscription of those who hospitably received and generously treated them when outcast and homeless, and of sectarian persecution of those who did not worship at the altar of their religious shrine; the repeated efforts of the Proprietary to reduce them to subjection, beginning with the memorable battle upon the Severn, and ending only with the turn of affairs in England, which took from them their moral support; the rise and fall of the intriguing and ambitious Fendall, the Cromwell of Maryland; the introduction of the printing press, that emblem of liberty which was not found in any other American Colony; the embroiling designs and the insurrection of the apostate Coode; the Protestant revolution of 1689; the fall of the Proprietary government; the administration of affairs by the representatives of the Crown, and the establishment of the Church of England, by law, in the province, all pass in review, and stand in "characteristic light and shade" upon its historic panorama.

On the ninth of June, 1647, Governor Leonard Calvert, at the early age of forty, died at St. Mary's, where his remains still repose under its revered and holy soil. Of the life and character of Leonard Calvert, historians have said but little. While there is no desire to detract from the unfading lustre which they have accorded to the Proprietaries of Maryland, truth and justice alike demand, that, of the pioneer Governor of the Province, and the founder of St. Mary's, it should here be said, that, he, who left his native land to lead the pilgrim colony to Maryland; he, who faced the perils and dangers and stood the heat and fire of storm and battle which so often darkened its early colonial days; he, who first proclaimed, and laid in practice those fundamental principles which underlie the priceless boon of liberty of conscience; he, who, with untiring energy, fidelity and zeal, devoted the best years of his life to the development and glory of Maryland, and to the prosperity and happiness of its citizens; he, whose undaunted courage and wise and liberal statesmanship, are so closely associated with the foundation, early growth and permanent establishment of Maryland, should stand upon the pages of history no less distinguished and renowned, as long as valiant service to early Maryland has an admirer, or civil and religious liberty a friend.

Of the Protestant Revolution of 1689, its causes and effects, and in which St. Mary's was the theatre of action, but little can be said within the limits of this address. Suffice it to say, that it resulted in the evacuation of St. Mary's, the downfall of the Proprietary government, the subjugation of Maryland by the Revolutionists, the assumption of political control of the Province by the Crown, and hence the establishment at St. Mary's of a royal government in Maryland, one of the first official acts of which, was that of overthrowing religious freedom—so long the pride of Maryland, and constituting, by law, the Church of England as the established church of the Province.

In 1694, Francis Nicholson, of Virginia, became Governor of Maryland, and signalized his induction into office by sounding the death knell of St. Mary's.

He summoned an Assembly to convene, not at St. Mary's, but at Anne Arundel Town, now Annapolis. This act "fore-shadowed the doom" of St. Mary's, and at that session of the Assembly the removal of the capital was determined upon.

The consternation which St. Mary's felt at this sudden, and to it, disastrous, movement, can well be understood. It solemnly protested, pathetically appealed and graciously offered through its mayor, recorder, aldermen and council, in which, after dwelling upon the ancient rights of the old city, sustained by long enjoyment and confirmed in the most solemn manner by Lord Baltimore, and upon the advantages of a site, with a commodious harbor and a beautiful and pleasant situation, they proposed to obviate its alleged difficulties of access, but all to no purpose. Governor Nicholson had moved the capital of Virginia from its ancient seat to Williamsburg, and had come to Maryland resolved upon the same course towards St. Mary's. He went through the form of submitting the address of the town officials to the

Assembly, from whence it was returned to him—whose wishes probably were well understood—with a reply conspicuous only for its vindictive spirit, bitter acrimony and extreme coarseness, in which they ridiculed the idea of being bound by proprietary promises, denied the advantages of St. Mary's, mocked at its calamities, laughed at its proposals, and scornfully declined further consideration of the subject.

In February, 1695, he ordered the archives and records to be removed from St. Mary's and to be delivered to the Sheriff of Anne Arundel Town. This was accordingly done, and on the 28th of February, 1695, the General Assembly began its first session at the present capital of Maryland.

The reason alleged for this change, was that St. Mary's, being on the verge of the Province, was difficult of access to the masses of the people. This may not have been altogether without weight, but it was more probably due to the fierce political struggle and the bitter sectarian strife, which existed there at that time—between the advocates of the Proprietary and the adherents of the King—between the church of England and the church of Rome.

It was, says Maryland's most eminent historian, McMahon, "the interest of the new government, to destroy, as far as possible, the cherished recollections which were associated with the departed Proprietary power; and there was no object so intertwined with all these recollections, as this ancient city, consecrated by the landing of the colonists, endeared to the natives as the first home of their fathers, and exhibiting at every step the monuments of that gentle and liberal administration, which had called up a thriving colony out of the once trackless wilderness. The Catholics of the colony dwelt principally in that section of it; and under the joint operation of these causes, it had been distinguished during all the troubles consequent upon the civil wars in England, by its unshaken attachment to the Proprietary. Without these considerations to prompt the removal, the recollections and the attachments, which centre the feelings of a people in an ancient capital, would probably have contributed to preserve it as such; until, by the denseness of the population, and the increasing facilities for traveling thereby afforded to the remote sections of the State, the objection to its location would have been in a great measure obviated, and the city of St. Mary's would at this day have been the seat of our State government. The excitement of the moment made its claims to recollection cogent reasons for its destruction, and the public convenience came in as the sanction."

After St. Mary's ceased to be the capital of the Province, it soon began to decline. The removal of the government officials in itself, seriously diminished its population, and, in 1708, it ceased also to be the county seat of St. Mary's county, the last symbol of its official character. The same year it lost its privilege of sending delegates to the General Assembly, and soon after lost its rank as a city.

No longer the commercial emporium of the Province, with no manufacturing interests at that day to sustain its vitality, and completely stripped of its official importance, it was left without means of support. Its population gradually departed; its old fort sank to the level of the earth; its houses—one by one—fell to ruin, and in a comparatively short time nothing remained, save the old State House and a few of the more durable buildings, the latter used as homesteads for the farms into which the site of the old city became converted. In 1695, permission was given the Justices of St. Mary's county to use the State House for a court house and church, and in 1720, the title to it, and the "Public Lot," which contained about three acres, by Act of Assembly, became vested in the "Rector and Vestry of William and Mary Parish, and their successors, in fee simple, for the use of the Parish forever." It continued to be used as a church for more than a century; but, in 1829, this historic old building was pulled down and its material used in the construction of Trinity church, which stands nearby.

This old monument might well have been "spared all but the ravages of time"—and had it been saved from the sacrilege of man—it might to-day be standing to "point a moral" and "adorn the history" of the founders of Maryland.

The State House stood on "St. Mary's bluff," which formed the northwestern extremity of the town. It was a strikingly beautiful situation and commanded an extensive view of the town, the river and the surrounding country; and to those approaching the city, either by land or water, it formed a prominent and picturesque feature of the landscape. Its dimensions were forty-five by fifty feet, its architectural design that of a maltese cross, and was one of the most pretentious public buildings of its time. It was built of large, red vitrified brick, its walls varying from twenty-eight to nineteen inches, diminishing in thickness with their height, the lower floor being divided into two halls for the accommodation of the upper and lower Houses of Assembly, and which were paved with flagstone. It was two and a half stories high, with steep roof covered with red tile, from the centre of which shot up an iron spire, with ball, supporting near its top, a vane, on which was inscribed, "1676," the date of its erection. The building, with a jail, cost 330,000 pounds of tobacco. By a singular coincidence, it was built without chimneys, owing to a controversy over the proposition to allow it, in conformity with the custom of the times, to be used as an ordinary or eating house, the opposing and predominant faction, in order to make this impracticable, caused them to be omitted altogether; and it was not until two years later, that its three massive outside chimneys were added, at a cost of 20,000 pounds of tobacco.

On the "State House Square," about seventy feet distant, stood the historic "Old Mulberry," under whose broad-spreading branches the first colonists of Maryland assembled, and under which also traditionary history says, the first mass at St. Mary's was celebrated and the treaty between Governor Calvert and the Yaocomico Indians was made. Of this venerable tree, whose mass of foliage continued for two hundred years afterward to crown the State House promontory, it is further recorded, that "on it were nailed the proclamations of Calvert and his successors, the notices of punishments and fines, the inventories of debtors whose goods were to be sold, and all notices calling for the public attention." Within comparatively recent years, even curious relic-hunters were able to pick from its decaying trunk the rude nails which thus "held the forgotten State papers of two centuries ago."

This aged tree had watched over the city in its infancy, in its development and prosperity, and in its pride and glory as the metropolis of Maryland; it had seen it stripped of its prestige and its honors, and lose its importance and its rank; it had witnessed its battle with adversity and its downfall and decline; and it had mourned the departure of nearly every symbol of its existence and memorial of its glory, which under the winning game of time had one by one faded and passed away; and still it stood—stood, as a "silent sentinel" of time whose "watchword is death;" stood, daily distilling the "dews of Heaven, upon the sacred ground around it; stood, sheltering the generations of men who were buried beneath its luxuriant shade; stood, telling the story of the first capital of Maryland, and marking the spot where once it was—stood until 1876, when, like the almost forgotten city, the companion of its prime, its time-worn and shattered trunk laid down to rest.

About fifteen feet from the site of the State House, stands what is known as the "Calvert Vault," and which is supposed to contain the remains of Governor Leonard Calvert, Lady Jane, the wife of Charles Lord Baltimore, and Cecilius, their oldest son. Of this vault, tradition says, its entrance was covered up and the key thrown into the river, that its revered inmates might peacefully repose forever, under the soil they had redeemed from the wilderness.

In 1839, the State of Maryland purchased from William and Mary Parish the eastern half of the State

House lot, and to commemorate the spot where "civilization and christianity were first introduced into our State," erected on it the imposing and classic building, known as the "St. Mary's Female Seminary." It also, a little more than two years ago, did tardy justice to Maryland's first Governor—Leonard Calvert—by erecting to his memory a handsome granite shaft, placing it on the site of the "old Mulberry;" and, at the same time, in order to perpetuate the foundation lines of the old State House, planted at each of its sixteen corners a massive granite marker.

Thus did the ancient city of St. Mary's spring into being, flourish and pass away. In the "very State to which it gave birth;" in the State whose foundations it erected; in the State, many of whose most valued institutions, and more ancient principles of organic law, it established, it to-day stands almost a "solitary spot, dedicated to God and a fit memento of perishable man."

But it is one, which, "as long as civilization shall endure upon the earth, will be memorable in the history of its development. The philosopher and the statesman, when tracing back the progress of the political systems of men from the loftiest heights they shall ever reach, will always pause upon the banks of the St. Mary's to contemplate one of the greatest epochs in their history. Here, under the auspices of the founders of the State of

Maryland, the injured freedom of England found a refuge from the depredations of royal power; here, the inherent rights of man found opportunity for growth to strength and vigor, away from the depressing tyranny of Kings; here, the ancient privileges of the people that came down with the succeeding generations of our fathers from the morning twilight of Anglo-Saxon history, struggling through the centuries with varying fortunes, at last found a home and a country as all-pervading as the atmosphere around them; here, these principles and rights first entered into the practical operations of government; here, was established the first State in America where the people were governed by laws made by themselves; here, was organized the first civil government in the history of the Christian world, which was administered under that great principle of American liberty—the independence of church and state in their relations to each other; here too, freedom of conscience, in all of its breadth and fullness, was first proclaimed to men as their inherent and inviolable right, in tones which, sounding above the tempest of bigotry and persecution, were to continue forever, from age to age, to gladden the world with the assurance of practical Christian charity, and ultimately find expression in the political systems of every civilized people."

Such was the halo surrounding Maryland's early colonial metropolis, and yet the present generation asks when and where it was; such the renown of Maryland's first capital, embodying in its history the germ of so much of that which gave grandeur and glory, as well as inspiration and pride, to the later annals of the State, and yet history has recorded its birth without a smile, and has written its epitaph without a tear.

In desolation and ruin as it is, and though its hearthstone is buried beneath the moss of so many years, it should be revered as a hallowed spot sacred to the "proudest memories" of Maryland; endeared in the pride and in the affection of its sons and its daughters; the glory of every American patriot, for it was the spot where first arose the radiant morning sun of our religious freedom; the spot where first broke and brightened into effulgent daylight the early dawn of our civil liberty.

SCRIPTURE READING AND PRAYER.

By Rev. Wm. S. Southgate, D. D.,
Rector of St. Anne's Church, Annapolis.

Delivered in the Hall of the House of Delegates, March 5, 1894, at the Celebration Ceremonies of that date.

READING.

The Lord our God be with us, as He was with our fathers. Let Him not leave us, nor forsake us; that He may incline our hearts unto Him, to walk in all His ways, and to keep His commandments, and His statutes, and His judgments, which He commanded our fathers. (I Kings, viii, 57-58.)

PRAYER.

Almighty God, our Heavenly Father, who art always more ready to hear than we to pray, and art wont to give more than either we desire or deserve; pour down upon us the abundance of Thy mercy. Forgive us those things whereof our conscience is afraid, and give us those good things which we are not worthy to ask, but through the merits and mediation of Jesus Christ, Thy Son, our Lord. We beseech Thee, O God, save and bless our State. Give wisdom and power for good to our Governor, our

Judges, the Senators and Delegates of the General Assembly, and to all others to whom is entrusted the authority of government. Grant that all their doings, being ordered by Thy governance, may be righteous in Thy sight, and for the good of all the people.

Bless our land with honorable industry, sound learning and pure manners. Defend our liberties, preserve our unity. Save us from violence, discord and anarchy; from pride and arrogance and every evil way. Fashion into one happy people the multitude brought here out of many kindreds and tongues.

Give us peace at home, and enable us to keep our high place among the nations of the earth. In the time of our prosperity temper our self-confidence with thankfulness, and, in the day of trouble, suffer not our trust in Thee to fail. Direct us, O Lord, now and ever, in all our doings, with Thy most gracious favor, and further us with Thy continual help; that, in all our works, begun, continued, and ended in Thee, we may glorify Thy holy name, and finally, by Thy mercy, obtain everlasting life, through Jesus Christ, our Lord. *Amen.*

REMARKS

OF

THOMAS S. BAER, Esq.,

On opening the proceedings in the Hall of the House of Delegates, on March 5th, 1894, in honor of the Bi-Centennial of the Removal of the Capital from St. Mary's to Annapolis.

It is one of the complaints of Ruskin against our country, that we have no antiquities. We have met to-night, to consider such antiquities as we have. To the citizen of the old world, two hundred years may seem a very short period in the history of a people, but on the virgin soil of the new world, it has witnessed the development of the most powerful nation on the globe. The special occasion which brings us together, is the 200th anniversary of the removal of the Capital of this State from St. Mary's to Annapolis. The town, from which the removal took place, has become so old, that it has disappeared from view more entirely than Thebes or Palmyra, while the young Arundel town, then proud of its new born dignity, is now widely known as the "Ancient City." On this historic spot, where, two hundred years ago, the first session of the Legislature in this city was held, the General Assembly has suspended, for the day, the business of the session, and has united with the municipal authorities of Annapolis to celebrate the event. These are the closing exercises in connection with the celebration. We meet to look back at the conditions that led to the removal of the Capital, to listen to the lament of those who, with saddened hearts, foresaw in that event, the beginning of decay, which ended in utter desolation, and to the rejoicings of those who felt that the establishment of the Capital here gave assurance of permanent prosperity.

But above the interest, which attaches to the mere event itself, it is fitting that we should let the occasion serve to recall who the founders of our colony were, the conditions under which the settlement was made and maintained, and to trace the beginning and growth of that spirit of freedom in civil government and in religious belief, which, when the fullness of time had come, sent the wisest of Maryland's sons to the Continental Congress, to participate in the creation of the great Republic, and the bravest to the field, to stay there until that Republic was recognized by the Mother Country.

It is my simple function, to-night, to introduce to you the gentlemen, through whom we are to look backward two centuries in the history of our beloved State.

When they shall have performed their tasks, and the work of the present shall be resumed, let us look forward, and "nobly resolve" that the plant of civil and religious liberty, which our fathers planted and tended with such solicitude and devotion, shall continue to bloom in consummate beauty during the centuries to come.

REMOVAL OF THE CAPITAL FROM ST. MARY'S TO ANNAPOLIS,

A Paper read, by invitation of the City of Annapolis, by

ELIHU S. RILEY,

At the Ceremonies in the Hall of the House of Delegates, on March 5, 1894, in honor of the Two Hundredth Anniversary of the Removal of the Capital from St. Mary's to Annapolis.

GENTLEMEN OF THE GENERAL ASSEMBLY AND FELLOW-CITIZENS:

Comparisons may be odious, but they are the searchlights of truth. The age, in which men and States lived, is the only background that will sharply define their characters to posterity.

When, by the camera of history, the silhouettes of contemporaneous events are thrown upon the canvas of time, then the chaste figure of Maryland shines like a star in the firmament of heaven.

The day when the Pilgrim Fathers of Maryland landed at St. Clements, was the age of blood, intolerance, and persecution. The Church militant, no longer hidden in the catacombs of Rome, from the faggots of Nero, had buckled on the sword of persecution, and was putting to its keen edge all who dared raise voice against hierarchical decree or sacerdotal authority.

This spirit belonged to no sect and to no denomination—to no party, and no creed it was the age—the age of a terrestrial Infernes. The very demons incarnate, from the bottomless pit, seemed to have been let loose in the scriptural Babylon.

Hus had been burned; Savonarola destroyed; the bones of St. Thomas a Becket exhumed and burned; the ashes of Wycliffe scattered to the sea; Charles the First executed; an epoch when Thomas Cromwell, as minister to Henry the Eighth, gave the order for the trial and place of execution of offenders in one and the same paper; a period when every misfortune to an evil-doer was hailed with sanctimonious delight by the faithful as a just judgment of Almighty God for his impiety; it was an age when Catholics in England were not allowed to hold office; nor import the insignia of their faith; nor educate their children abroad in the principles of their religion; nor receive the rights of their church in their own land, nor even inherit the property of their parents. Laud, Archbishop of Canterbury, had been slain by the Presbyterians, and John Ogilvie, Jesuit, had been executed at Glasgow for high treason, for holding adverse opinion to the government and in saying MASS.

Sir Thomas More's trial displays the spirit of the times in all their error and severity. "The charge contained in the indictment was—1, that the prisoner had stubbornly opposed the King's second marriage; 2, that he maliciously refused to declare his opinion of the act of supremacy (the act that made Henry VIII head of the church of England); 3, that he endeavored to evade the force of that statute, and advised Bishop Fisher, by his letters, not to submit to it; and 4, that upon his examination in the *Tower*, it being demanded, if he approved the act of supremacy, he answered, *that the question was like a two-edged sword; if he answered one way, it would destroy his body; and if the other way, his soul;* and these were said to be open or overt acts *of treason of the heart*," and Sir Thomas was accordingly executed.

In the new world matters were no better. As late as 1662, in Massachusetts, Quakers were whipped whenever they could be found delivering their message. Men and women were tied to cart's tails, and scourged from town to town, and so it happened in New Hampshire, then a part of the bay.

In Cambridge, a woman was thrown into jail without food or bedding. A Quaker brought her some milk; he was fined five pounds and put in the same jail.

"The cases of these persecutions," says Mr. Bryant, "are too numerous to mention singly, and they all have a revolting sameness. They lasted ten years, and did not come to an end until the King, offended by the prohibition of Episcopacy, and of the reading of the Liturgy, issued sharp injunctions against them."

Wilson and Robinson, previous to these minor cruelties, had been executed for the innocent offence of preaching the mild religion of the Quakers; Margaret Jones and Anne Hibbens hanged as witches; Roger Williams driven to the wilderness for proclaiming liberty of conscience; and the Salem Witchcraft horror was in course of evolution in the laboratory of bigotry, superstition, and pious fanaticism.

Bryant, in telling the story of Connecticut, says: "Women were stripped for a whipping, one of them was whipped with a lately born babe clinging to her breast, and the record of fining, starving, imprisoning, banishing and miscellaneous cruelty becomes monotonous."

Virginia Churchmen could not brook even the dissenter, and their harsh laws, rigorously enforced in 1648, drove the Puritan from the Old Dominion.

From this sea of terror and merciless atrocities, arises the form of one that reflects the spirit of a new-born, heaven-inspired civilization. History will vindicate the assertion that George Calvert was the greatest man of his age—great in the pure nobility of his sturdy character, great in the wisdom of his stupendous grasp, in an age of vindictive bigotry, of the sound problems of civil and constitutional government. He called a world's attention to the sublime truth that liberty of conscience, in matters of religion, was consonant with the loyalty of the subject to the highest or remotest interests of the State, and that that spot was most blest where no statute laws required obedience to creed, and that place in which these principles would have fair trial—WAS MARYLAND.

It was in splendid keeping with such sentiments that, when Churchmen drove the Puritan from Virginia, Catholic Maryland gave him asylum, and sealed the compact with the immortal act of 1649, which was the first original legislation on American soil, guaranteeing the rights of conscience and of religion.

It is revivifying to come, from time to time, to the springs of eternal truth, and there, rearing our altars of devotion, venerate the spirits of noble men, and drink in inspiration for duty, God and country. As Marylanders, let us once more read together this *magna charta* of Maryland liberties, wherein our sires made statute law, what had been the unwritten and common law of the province since its settlement:

"Chapter 1, Acts of 1649. Cæcilius, Lord Baltimore, William Stone, governor.

"And whereas, the enforcing of the conscience in matters of religion, hath frequently fallen out to be of dangerous consequence in those Commonwealths, where it hath been practised, and for the more quiet and peaceable government of this province, and the better to preserve mutual love and unity among the inhabitants, no person or persons whatsoever, within this province, or the Islands, ports, harbours, creeks or havens, thereunto belonging, professing to believe in JESUS CHRIST, shall from henceforth be any way troubled, molested, or discountenanced, for, or in respect of his or her religion, nor in the free exercise thereof, within this province, or the Islands thereunto belonging, nor any way compelled to the belief or exercise of any other religion, against his or her consent, so as they be not unfaithful to the Lord Proprietary, or molest or conspire against the Civil Government established or to be established in this province, under him or his heirs. And any person presuming contrary to this act and the true intent and meaning thereof, directly or indirectly, either in person or estate, wilfully to disturb, wrong, trouble, or molest, any person whatsoever, within this province, professing to believe in JESUS CHRIST, for or in respect of his or her religion, or the free exercise thereof, within this province, otherwise than is provided for in this act, shall pay treble damage to the party so wronged and molested, and also forfeit 20 shillings sterling for every such offence, one-half to his Lordship, the other half to the party molested, and, in default of paying the damage or fine, be punished by public whipping and imprisonment, at the pleasure of the Lord Proprietary."

It rang out like the peal of liberty bells on this dark night of cruelty and intolerance, and was neither cant nor dead letter, for, as long as Lord Baltimore was preserved in his rights, there freedom of conscience was guaranteed, and our ancient court-rolls contain the record that Capt. William Lewis, Catholic, was fined for contemptuously speaking of the religion of his Protestant servants.

Nor are the praises of the liberal spirit of our forefathers left to our own State historians.

Lord Baltimore "laid," says Chalmers, "the foundation of this province upon the broad basis of security to property and of freedom to religion, granting in absolute fee fifty acres of land to every emigrant; establishing Christianity agreeably to the old common law, of which it is a part, without allowing pre-eminence to any particular sect. The wisdom of his choice soon converted a dreary wilderness into a prosperous colony."

Judge Story, in his Commentaries, speaking of the same subject, the colonization of Maryland, which antedated the Act of Toleration fifteen years, says: "It is certainly very honorable to the liberality and public spirit of the proprietary, that he should have introduced into his fundamental policy the doctrine of general toleration and equality among Christian sects, and have thus given the earliest example of a legislator inviting his subjects to the free indulgence of religious opinion. This was anterior to the settlement of Rhode Island, and therefore merits the enviable rank of being the first recognition amongst the colonists of the glorious and indefeasible rights of conscience."

William Cullen Bryant, in his History of the United States, wrote: "Enough remains of the annals of Lord Baltimore's colony to show most plainly those distinctive features which separated its founders *sharply from all the other strongly-marked* types, from which the varying races of the future nation sprang. Here were men trained in a different school from New Englanders or Virginians; men with a singular mixture of religious enthusiasm, culture, practical shrewdness and liberal statesmanship, far enough in advance of their age to take warning from the errors of others, and, while they founded a province in which were mingled feudal and popular, despotic and constitutional institutions, to administer it with such prudence that it grew strong and gained permanence more quickly and tranquilly than any of its predecessors."

Says the learned Bancroft: "Sir George Calvert deserves to be ranked among the wisest and most benevolent law givers, for he connected his hopes of the aggrandizement of his family with the establishment of popular institutions, and, being a papist, 'wanted not charity toward Protestants.'

"Toleration grew up in the province silently as a custom of the land. Through the benignity of the administration, no person professing to believe in the divinity of Jesus Christ was permitted to be molested on account of religion. Roman Catholics, who were oppressed by the laws of England, were sure to find an asylum on the north bank of the Potomac; and there, too, Protestants were sheltered against Protestant intolerance. From the first, men of foreign birth enjoyed equal advantages with those of the English and Irish nations."

As these Virginia Puritans turned their faces toward the fair land of Mary, they saw there the flower of liberty blooming in the full fragrance of its primeval creation; and here they found refuge on this very spot, on which we are gathered to-night, and aptly and reverently called it "PROVIDENCE."

This was in 1649.

Historians and intelligent men of all professions have been justly interested in the religious denominations of the men who laid the corner-stone and builded the fair walls of our State on such broad and most Christian basis.

The proprietary and the majority of the first colonists were Catholics, but, in mutual love and respect, a goodly, though unknown, number of Protestants, united with them to lay the head of the corner deep in the eternal principles of constitutional and religious liberty; it was a Catholic Proprietary and a Catholic House of Burgesses that passed the act of toleration, but a Protestant Governor, who was undoubtedly largely instrumental in its enactment, three Protestant councillors, all appointed by a Catholic Proprietary, making, with the Governor, a majority of the Upper House, and a Protestant minority in the House of Burgesses, assented to it. Thus, to their everlasting honor be it said, to Catholic belongs the chief glory of both deeds, yet, in the union of Churchman and Catholic, as they had laid the corner-stone, and, side by side, reared the pillars of the temple of liberty, so, the splendid renown of these twin deeds of immortal fame, that flashed like new creations in celestial space, outstrips the confines of sects and denominations, and belongs to all Marylanders; for these noble men were our forefathers; their blood courses in our veins; and the honor of their deeds descends alike to every Marylander as a part of his magnificent heritage.

One witch only hanged is the sole case in Maryland, in all this bloody night of insane and relentless persecution, and one Quaker driven from the province by the

Puritans of Providence, for refusing to take the oath of allegiance. These told, and set against that dynasty of terrors, is this matchless antithesis—in all the reigns of the three Lords Baltimore, a period of over sixty years, when persecution reddened every other quarter of the globe, not one single individual, Jew or Gentile, was ever molested in Maryland for worshipping his God according to the dictates of his conscience; for, although the act of toleration limited religious liberty to Christians, the common and unwritten law extended, from the founding of the colony, its ægis to all mankind of every religious faith.

Have we not right to thank God for this record, and laud and magnify the men who made it, regardless of their creed?

Like the sentries at night along the Potomac, after a day of battle, during our mighty war between the States, who exchanged the tobacco of one for the coffee of the other, and discussed with fraternal feelings the conflict of the day, so we approach, with candor and fairness, the eventful annals which caused our ancestors the debate severe, the loss of valuable privileges, the roar of battle, and the sacrifice of heroes.

In them all, the halo of honor that surrounds the chronicles of our State, increases in brilliancy as we draw nigh the temples of our history, and inspect with keener vision the noble lives of Maryland men, and place the annals of Maryland's colonists alongside contemporaneous American settlements, or challenge even the records of time itself to present a land larger in liberality than that founded by the Prilgrim Fathers of Maryland.

It was in that day, the only spot in all the world where man "might worship God according to the dictates of his conscience, none daring to molest or make him afraid."

Lord Baltimore anticipated his times a hundred years, when he required his officers to swear that they "would not directly or indirectly trouble, molest or discountenance any person whatsoever in the said province, professing to believe in Jesus Christ."

The quarrels of the old world were shut out of the new, and Maryland became the "Land of the Sanctuary," where Friend and Puritan, Catholic and Churchman, dwelt together in happiness, pursued the avocations of peace, and rendered unto God the adoration of their consciences according to the forms of their faith and practice.

Able to cope with his colonial foes, so long as they confined their contests to questions belonging exclusively to the new world, Lord Baltimore found himself powerless to meet his enemies whenever they raised their banners crimsoned with the battles of internecine warfare in England, or waived the standard of Old World, religious dissensions within the borders of the province. Claiborne and Coode yielded to his superior force and the might of right, but Bennett, championing the cause of Cromwell, and Coode, the rights of William and Mary, brought the sceptre of the Lord of Avalon and the Proprietary of Maryland, to the dust, and, with its fall, the "Land of the Sanctuary" became a pandemonium of persecution.

Such was the anterior history of Maryland, such the era of atrocity in which the State had birth; and these were the primary causes that led to the removal of the capital of Maryland from St. Mary's to Annapolis.

Planted on any site, however inappropriate, a capital immediately throws out its tendrils, and takes root in the affections and traditions of the commonwealth. Deeper in the soil of the body politic, time thrust these roots, and diminishes the chances of their transplanting. History establishes the fact that capitals are not lightly removed from one place to another, and that a State clings to the site of its ancient seat of government with almost religious veneration.

Maryland has had but two substantial changes of its capital. Several temporary removals have taken place, but from 1634, the year of the settlement of the colony, to 1683, St. Mary's remained legally, and, most of the time, really, the venerated capital of Maryland.

The first proof St. Mary's had that this treasured prerogative could be wrested from her, was in 1654, after the Commissioners of Parliament had reduced the colony to obedience to the Commonwealth, to which authority, indeed, it had never been disobedient. The General Assembly, called by the Puritan authorities, met at one Richard Preston's house, on the Patuxent river, to which place the documents and records of the colony had been removed. In 1656, whilst St. Mary's remained the official residence of Lord Baltimore's Lieutenant in the Province, Gov. Fendall, Patuxent still continued the place of the regular meeting of the General Assembly. St. Mary's, in the year 1659, was fully restored to her ancient prerogatives, and, in that year, the session of the General Assembly was held there.

St. Mary's remained undisturbed in her re-acknowledged honors until 1683, when through the remoteness of the town from the rest of the province, its inconvenience and expense of access, which had always been "felt and often complained of," it was once more temporarily shorn of its laurels. The will of the Proprietary and feelings of the people had conspired to sustain the privileges of this ancient city; but the former, in 1683, yielded to the desires of a discontented people, and the Assembly was removed, with the courts and provincial offices, to a place called "the Ridge," in Anne Arundel county. One session only of the General Assembly was held there. The poor accommodations of the Ridge drove them hence, and the peripatetic capital took up its abode on Battle Creek, on the Patuxent River, from whence, after a session of three days only, it was again removed to its old site, St. Mary's. The Provincial Court found it necessary also to adjourn from the Ridge from want of accommodations.

Once more settled at St. Mary's, the Proprietary gave the inhabitants a written promise that the capital "should not be removed again during his life." Resting under this assurance, the people of St. Mary's had reason to feel secure, for, at least, that uncertain period—a human life; but political events defy all human calculations.

Annapolis, yet called PROVIDENCE, had evinced a desire for the location of the seat of government within its limits very early in its history, for, in 1674, when the Legislature was considering the propriety of erecting a State House, prison, and office, at St. Mary's, a member of the lower house stated, and the house sent the message to the Governor and Council, that "there are several persons of qualitie in Anne Arundel county, that will undertake to build a State House, prison, and office, at *there* own charge, onlie to be repaid by the country, when the buildings are finished, and to build a house for his Excellency, at their own proper costs and charges." The

Lower House showed that it was fully ripe for the innovation by voting "that it be necessarie, and this house doe petition his excellencie accordingly." The Upper House gave a sharp reply. It considered the paper no answer to the captain-general's choice already expressed, and declared it not fit to take any further notice, "but that the Lower House be desired to signifie to this house of what dimensions the said buildings are to be, and then some persons will offer themselves as undertakers of the same."

In 1688, William of Orange mounted the throne of England, and Protestantism became the ascendant religion of that kingdom. Lord Baltimore received instructions to proclaim William and Mary, as sovereigns, in the province of Maryland. He promptly obeyed. His orders, however, failed to reach his agents in Maryland in proper season, and waiting to hear his mind in the matter, the Proprietary's "timid deputies lost him his government."

The instrument of the revolution was "an association in arms, for the defense of the Protestant religion, and for asserting the rights of King William and Queen Mary to the province of Maryland and all the English dominions." John Coode, a notorious malcontent, was the leader of the association. After a brief struggle, the association, in August, 1689, obtained entire possession of the province. A convention was immediately held in the name of the association, and a full account of the proceedings and purposes of the organization was submitted to the King. He approved the revolution, and the province was governed by the authority of the convention until April 9, 1692. At that time, in accordance with the wishes of the convention, Sir Loniel Copley, who had been appointed the first royal Governor of Maryland, assumed control of the affairs of the province. He convened the Legislature at once. Notwithstanding the Governor counselled moderation in legislation, the General Assembly commenced its work by throwing a fire-brand in the province, in thanking the King for redeeming them "from the arbitrary will and pleasure of a tyrannical Popish government under which they had so long groaned." This was, indeed, a most unwarrantable assertion.

The Protestant religion was established by law by the Legislature, and provision made for its support by general taxation. This was *the first State church in Maryland*. Lord Baltimore's agents were prohibited from collecting port duties, and the collection of his land rents was greviously interrupted.

The old city of St. Mary's, around which clustered all the historic associations of early settlement, was immolated, in turn, upon the altar of revolution. The town about this period, 1694, contained about sixty houses—a number it had reached a few years after its settlement. Stunted in its early energies, its vital powers were sapped, and, at the period when the removal of the capital was suggested, had become "a mere landing place for the trade of its own immediate neighborhood." St. Mary's had several disadvantages that presented the site unfavorably to the legislators. Situated at the southern extremity of the province, its remoteness, and the expense and inconvenience of reaching or leaving it, constantly annoyed those who had business in the "antient capital." Beside, it had another quality to discommend it to the chief rulers of that period,—its people were Catholics, whilst the legislators were peculiarly Protestant, at least, as far as those illiberal partizans could represent Protestant principles. With all these against St. Mary's, there is no surprise at the result.

The place contemplated as the new capital was the "Town at Proctors," now Annapolis. This city was not even as large as St. Mary's; but it was central and anti-Catholic. It had been created a town and port of entry, in 1683, and in 1694, was designated as "Anne Arundel Town," and was made the residence of the district collector, the naval officer, and their deputies "for the dispatch of shipping." In 1700, six years later, it was thus described: "Col. Nicholson, the Governor, has done his endeavor *to make a town* OF THAT PLACE. There are about forty dwellings in it, seven or eight of which can afford a good lodging or accommodations for strangers. There are also a State House and a free school, built of brick, which make a great show among a parcel of wooden houses, and the foundation of a church is laid, the only brick church in Maryland. They have two market days in a week; and had Gov. Nicholson continued there a few months longer, he had brought it to perfection."

The people of St. Mary's did not let this valued treasure slip from their grasp without making the most strenuous efforts to retain it. They turned their eyes toward Gov. Nicholson, lifted up their hands, and, casting themselves at his feet in an agony of desperation, as their only hope, prayed him for succor in this, the day of their great calamity. They directed a petition to him, as "His Excellency," and as "Captain, General and Governor-in-Chief, in, and over this, their Majesty's province and Territory of Maryland." The address began: "The Mayor, Recorder, Aldermen, Common Councilmen and Freemen of the city of St. Mary's in the said province, *and principally* from the bottom of their hearts, they rejoice in your Excellency's happy accession to this, your Government; and sincerely pray for your peaceable and quiet enjoyment thereof, and long and prosperous continuance therein for the Glory of

God, their Majesty's service, the good and benefit of their subjects, and your own particular comfort and satisfaction."

The petitioners then supplicate the Governor to continue "their ancient franchises, rights and privileges, granted them by their charter, with such other benefits and advantages as hath been accustomed and generally allowed, and, from time to time, continued to them by your predecessors, rulers and governors of the province, humbly offering and proposing to your Excellency these following reasons as motives inducing thereto.

These were classed under sixteen heads:

"*Imprimus*, as that it was the prime and original settlement of the province, and from the first seating thereof, for above sixty years, hath been the antient and chief seat of Government."

The second reason was that Lord Baltimore had conferred on it, in consideration of the above fact, especial privileges.

The third paragraph set forth that the Capital should remain where it was, because "the situation in itself is most pleasant and healthful and naturally commodious in all respects for the purpose, being plentifully and well watered with good and wholesome springs, and almost encompassed around with harbor for shipping, where five hundred sail of ship, at least, may securely ride at anchor before the city." The town also contained, this section asserted, excellent points of land, on which to erect fortifications to defend said shipping, and for the preservation of the "public magazine and records of the province."

The fourth argument recited that the Capital ought not to be removed, because, by an act of the Legislature of 1662, land was bought, and, in 1674, the Legislature passed an act to build a State House and a prison, which cost the province 300,000 pounds of tobacco; and the next asserted that the inhabitants of St. Mary's had made a free-will offering of 100,000 pounds of tobacco to build Lord Baltimore a house adjacent to the town.

The sixth and seventh paragraphs recounted the removal to the Ridge in 1683, and those inconveniences that brought again the Capital to the "antient seat of government."

The eighth reason given was that, for the encouragement of the inhabitants to make provision for all who would be called to the Capital, Lord Baltimore promised that the seat of government should not be removed from St. Mary's during his life.

The ninth section states that "upon which encouragement given, several of the inhabitants of the said city *have launched out*, disbursed considerable estates to their great impoverishment and almost utter ruin, if they should be defeated of such, their promised encouragement, and not only so, but divers others, the inhabitants for several miles about, contiguous and adjacent to the said county, upon the same encouragement of his Lordship, have seated themselves upon mean and indifferent lands, and laid out their estates, and made improvements thereon, barely for the raising of stock wherewith to supply said city for the end and purpose aforesaid, which is now become their whole and only dependence for their future support and maintenance."

The tenth paragraph depicted the advantages of St. Mary's—its convenience for masters of vessels and others coming in and going out of the province, the dispatch of letters and expresses, its accessibleness from Patuxent and Potomac rivers, and the Main Bay, beside the colony of Virginia, "with whom mutual intercourse and correspondence is most undeniably necessary and material."

The eleventh reason announced that the Capital should not be removed, because Governor Copley had been required to enter upon his gubernatorial duties at St. Mary's.

The twelfth set forth, "that scarce any precedent can be produced of so sudden a change as the removal of the antient and chief seat of government, *upon the careless suggestion and allegation of some particular persons for their own private interest and advantage,*" and to array Governor Nicholson upon the side of St. Mary's, the petitioners flattered him with the soft impeachment that the removal of the Capital was invested with him as their majesty's representative, and, at his Excellency's feet, "continued the petitioners, *we humbly cast ourselves for relief and support against the calamities and ruin wherewith we are threatened*, and wholly relying upon your Excellency's grace and favor therein, with whom, we also conceive, should be good manners, in all persons, first to treat and intercede, before they presume to make any peremptory result, in case of so high a nature as this may be."

The 13th and 14th paragraphs reminded the Governor that, in 1692, "it was put to the vote of *a full house*, whether the holding of the courts and assembly at St. Mary's were a grievance, or not, and carried in the negative," and the petitioners "humbly conceive that house did well consider all difficulties and outlays, losses and expenses to be incurred in moving the Capital, besides the hazards and casualties of removing and transporting the records from one place to another, of which already some experience hath been had."

To meet all objections of inconvenience of travel, the petitioners offered to provide, as soon as possible, "a coach or caravan, or both, to go at all times of public meeting of Assemblies and Provincial Courts, and so forth, every day, daily, between St. Mary's and Patuxent river, and, at all other times, once a week; and also to keep constantly on hand a dozen horses, at least, with suitable furniture, for any person or persons, having occasion to ride post, or otherwise, with or without a guide, to any port of the province on the Western Shore."

The sixteenth section suggested that the objection that St. Mary's was not in the centre of the province, and, therefore, not suitable as the capital, was conspicuously untenable from the fact that the Imperial Court is held in London, "as far from the centre of England as St. Marie's in this province; Boston, in New England; Port Royal, in Jamaica; Jamestown, in Virginia; and almost all other, their Majestic's American plantations, where are still kept and continued in their first antient stations and places, the chief seat of government and courts of judicature."

To this were subscribed the names of the Mayor, Aldermen and Councilmen of St. Marie's, with the freemen thereof, among the latter being that of JOHN COODE, the leader of the revolution that was to take from St. Mary's its chief glory—another proof that we may start revolutions, but we cannot stop them.

Then followed an especial sop for the Governor, in which the same parties hoped that the reasons and motives herewith offered to his Excellency and the Council, will prevent their assent to the contemplated law, and affirmed that they placed their reliance on "his Excellency's known experience, assisted by so worthy a Council." They urged again that it was a royal prerogative only to change the seat of Government, and when that authority was invaded, "the State is in a confusion." Knowing their Majestie's respect for the rights of their subjects, as "sufficiently evidenced by their placing *a person of your Excellency's known regard to the same at the helm of the Government*, the petitioners do humbly conceive that it is not consistent with the rules of gratitude for so great a blessing, as to pass a law which, your petitioners are well-informed, is an apparent incroachment upon their Majesty's prerogative."

A prayer, appended to this lengthy review of the case, *showed* how solicitous the people of St. Mary's were for the reputation of the State. "Least," said they, "the province may be so blamed as to have it said that it was the first of the American plantations, that offered violence to the prerogative of so worthy a prince." They asked that the Governor will reject the bill, until, at least, leave be first obtained from his Majesty. "An apology, for putting, with so much freedom, his Excellency in mind of a matter which they knew was his chiefest care to preserve," concludes the paper.

The Governor sent the petition to the Lower House. A quaint and jeering reply was returned by the House. It was:

"By the Assembly, Oct. the 11th, 1694.

"This House have read and considered of the petitions and reasons of the Mayor, Aldermen and others, calling themselves Common Council and Freemen of the City of St. Marie's, against removing the Courts and Assembly of, from this corner and poorest place in the province, to the centre and best abilitated place thereof. Although wee conceive the motives there laid downe, are hardly deserving any answer at all, many of them being *against the plain* matter of fact, some against reason, and all against Generall good and wellfaire of the province; yet, because your excellency has been pleased to lay them before us, wee humbly returne this our sense of the same, that, as to the 1st, 2d, 3d, 4th, 5th, 6th, 7th and 8th reasons, relating to what his Lord Proprietary has thought fitt to do to the City of St. Marie's, it is no Rule nor Guide to their Majesties, your Excellency, nor this house. *It seems in some parts to reflect* on his Lord Proprietary more than this house believes is true, or deserved by his Lord Proprietary.

"2d. As to the 9th: This house say that it is against the plain matter of fact, for wee can decerne noe estate, either laid out, or to lay out in, or about this famous city, comparable with other parts of this province. But they say, and can make appeare that there has been more money spent here, by three degrees, or more, than this city and all the inhabitants for tenn miles round is worth, and say that, having had 60ty-odd years of experience of this place, and almost a quarter part of the province devoured by it, and still, like Pharoah's kine, remain as at first, they are discouraged to add any more of their substance to such ill-improvers.

"As to the tenth and eleventh, wee conceive the being of St. Maries soe near Virginia, is not soe great an advantage to the province, as the placeing the courts in the centre and richest part of the same, which is noe great distance thence of Virginia either, and nearer New York and other Governments which we have as much to doe with as Virginia, if not more, and the place as well watered and commodious in all respects as St. Maries, which has only served hither to cast a Blemish upon all the rest of the province in the Judgment of all discerning strangers, who, perceiving the meanness of the head, must rationally judge proportionably of the body thereof.

"To the 12th, 13th and 14th, they say that they do not hold themselves accountable to the Mayor and his Brethren for what they doe for their country's service, nor by what measures they do the same, nor what time they shall take to doe it in, nor for what reasons; and are, and will be, as carefull of the records and properties of the people, as the proprietary.

"To the 15th, the house say the petitioners offer faire as they have done formerly; but never yet performed any, and this house believes that the general welfare of the province ought to take place of that sugar plum of all the Mayor's coaches, who, as yet, has not one.

"To the 16th, this house conceive that the citty of St. Maries is very unequally rankt with London, Boston, Port Royall, &c.

"All which wee humbly offer to your Excellency's juditious consideration."

All the honeyed words of flattery that fell from the lips of the petitioners upon the ear of "his Excellency," were also unavailing. On receiving the answer of the House of Delegates, the Council tersely recorded its view of the matter in this brief paragraph: "This Board concur with the said answers made by the House of Burgesses."

The removal was consummated the ensuing winter, and the Assembly met first on the 28th of February, 1694, (old style,) in its new Capital.

St. Mary's will ever remain holy ground to all mankind. Here, amid the darkness of relentless persecution for the right of conscience, that covered every other spot of the globe, was the one altar of liberty raised, and the lamp of freedom lit, that illumed "the Land of the Sanctuary,"—a beacon light to all the world—the Day-Star of American freedom itself.

No people has a nobler heritage than Marylanders, and as St. Mary's is conspicuous as the shekinah of human conscience, so Annapolis became the living embodiment of aggressive defence of American liberty against every encroachment of royal prerogative, for, from the assembling of the first authorized Legislature, at St. Mary's, in 1638, when the House of Burgesses wrung from the grasp of the proprietary, the right to initiate its own laws, down to the day articles of peace with Great Britain were ratified by Congress in the Senate Chamber of Maryland, in 1784, and Maryland's early example of liberty became the blessed heritage of all the States, no body of men, any where in the American colonies, was more steadfastly alert and courageous in asserting its rights as British citizens, and in support of the American Revolution, than our faithful representatives, the fearless members of the House of Delegates of Maryland.

THE CATHOLIC AND THE PURITAN SETTLER IN MARYLAND,

By Alfred P. Dennis, A. M.

An Address delivered on invitation of the Maryland Legislature, in the Hall of the House of Delegates, March 5, 1894, at the Celebration of the Bi-Centennial of the Removal of the State Capital from St. Mary's to Annapolis.

Ladies and Gentlemen:

It is most appropriate that the people of this immediate vicinity should publicly celebrate a day that chose this city above the fairest of her sisters, and exalted her to political headship. It is fitting that men selected for the honorable discharge of public duties should pause in the business of State to observe a day that rehearses the story of the first English colony governed by laws enacted in a provincial assembly. It is becoming that the citizens of a great commonwealth should commemorate an act which had its genesis in the resistance of a liberty-loving people to the paramount authority of an hereditary sovereign. Surrounded to-day by the progressive spirit of the western world, with its exhaustless material resources, its matchless achievements of thought, the appeal is made to the past, with all it has given, with all it gives, as a pledge and inspiration for the future. If the records unearthed and deciphered by the Geologist have forced us to add countless ages to the life of mankind, they have robbed us of a fair proportion of boasted antiquity. And yet our wholesome consciousness of the forces that gather by duration and persistence, loses nothing of its potency because our citizenship is cast in a land which antiquity rightly styles the "New World." Better a generation of political life, where an awakening human conscience has thrown off the fetters of nature and broken the bonds of the despot, than forty centuries of an organized society that schools man in the one lesson that status has placed him irredeemably under the will of an inexorable master. Popular assemblies met in the Province of the Calverts before the independence of any existing Republic of the Old World had been acknowledged. Democratic institutions put forth their flower on the banks of the Chesapeake, when the weeds of a feudal absolutism still grew rank on European soil. Laws were old upon our statute books when the vast country beyond the Alleghanies was as little known, and thought as little worth knowing, as the heart of Africa. These laws had run a century's course when native and alien hosts joined in vain struggle to plant on American soil the lilies of France. As two centuries look down upon us to-day, from popular institutions planted on these shores, I point you not to a past that is dead, but to a past that lives. Our past is a record of life, life that has subdued the rough forces of nature; life that has braved a thousand perils and survived a thousand hardships; life that has persisted unquenchable through endless cycles of change, and survives abundantly to-day in the fuller development of a robust statehood. Royalty's fiction, that the King never dies, carries with it more than a half-truth. Generations pass away, society lives on. Human society is an organism, it grows from within, its roots lie deep in the past. It is not a contradiction to say that the individual may have an independent life, and at once be an expression of the general spirit of society.

A thousand vain experiments in political mechanics have shown that constitutions are not manufactured, but grow. A thousand dismal failures have shown that no political alchemy can transform the baser into the nobler metals to perform the function of money. A thousand wretched blunders have shown that legislative bodies cannot make that law which does not reflect the common consciousness of society. Our statute books are choked to-day with laws which have not kept pace with the life of the community, and are as dead as the hands that penned them, or with laws that have so far run ahead of the common habit that they are as idle as the cries of the heathen prophets of Baal. The "bare ruin'd choirs" of even a Shakespeare's life remind us that the individual existence is at best a short career, whose history from preface to conclusion is largely a record of ideals missed. Hope for humanity cannot be founded upon what any individual can accomplish as a disconnected unit. Like the coral reef that springs imperishable from ocean's depths, a monument to the countless toilers that gave their little lives in its construction, the organism which we call the state, has developed by successive increments through a hundred generations. The fleeting life of the unit has been built into the undying life of the aggregate. I purpose to-night to point out certain constructive elements built into the fabric of this commonwealth during the early and formative period of our colonial history.

The early colonizers of Maryland, though sprung from a common stock, were not a homogeneous people in their sympathies and antipathies. Maryland soil had been occupied by three distinct classes of settlers before the middle of the seventeenth century. Clayborne was first in the field with his Protestant settlement on Kent island. Profit, and not piety, was the greatest object in life for Clayborne. Pre emption, and not redemption, gave pith and purpose to his enterprise. Between these Church-of-England men, backed in their possession by fair legal claims, and the later Catholic settlers in St. Mary's, there was no more community of interest than is indicated in their armed conflict on the waters of the Chesapeake. Aside from the sporadic attempts of Clayborne to vindicate his property rights by arms, he and his band have no large formative influence in our early state life.

Nor was there more community of interest between the planters on the Potomac and the Puritan band that settled fifteen years later on the banks of the Severn. Five years had not run their course before Old World animosities had burst into a flame and plunged "Papist" and "Precisian" into the fiercer struggle of an appeal to arms. Distrust, prejudice, antipathy, doubly scaled the commission of every actor in this struggle, yet each party represented principles complemental and significant in the splendid development of civil and religious liberty in the Maryland Province. The Roman Catholic was tolerant in religion, but narrow in politics. The Puritan was narrow in religion, but in politics liberal. While historians have delighted to retouch the glowing picture of the religious toleration of the Roman Catholic colonists, the wholesome influence of these Puritan settlers in moulding the early political life of the Province has been largely ignored. They have been scouted as troublers of a well-ordered system—as Adullamites drawing into sympathy with themselves the disaffected, the chagrined, the Ishmael brood that takes to the wilderness in explosive self-assertion rather than endure identification with a regime as distasteful to them as was ever the party and partisans of Luther to Pascal, Fenelon and the brilliant company of Port Royal. It has been pointed out that these Catholics of St. Mary's were expatriated, harried out of their native land by a proud Anglican hierarchy and a parliament of Puritan temper. Assuredly upon the heads of the Protestants lies the base sin of ingratitude. Their example in religious matters becomes one of exclusiveness, narrowness and ban. Catholics were disfranchised in the colony they had planted. Nor did the movement stop until the seat of government had been transferred from Catholic St. Mary's to the spot on which we stand.

The more lurid tints of the foregoing picture fade in the light of closer investigation. A host of authorities contend that Maryland was intended as an asylum for Roman Catholics, who found upon the banks of the Potomac the Puritan Plymouth. This is the generally accepted view, yet this portion of our history remains to be rewritten. The Puritan settlers in Maryland, and *not* the Catholics, were religious refugees. When George Calvert projected his scheme of a Proprietary Colony across the sea, the Catholics—we use the term throughout in its popular meaning—in high good favor at Court, enjoyed a fuller indulgence than they had known for more than half a century. Granting for a moment that an asylum was needed, how explain the purpose of Calvert's Avalon Colony in Newfoundland, undertaken before his Catholic faith was considered worth the avowal? If refugees—how account for Calvert's attempt to settle in Virginia, where he would have encountered the church establishment from which he is supposed to have fled? If refugees—how account for a very considerable number of Protestants in the first expedition to Maryland? The theory can not stand. The purpose in the founding of the Maryland Colony by the Calverts was mainly economic, and not religious.

Any theory that may be accepted in explanation of Calvert's purpose in the colonization of Maryland leads by a natural regress of causes to England under the first of the Stuarts.

The dissolution of the monasteries by Henry VIII left the Church stricken and helpless. From this point may be dated the downfall of the Catholic hierarchy in England. The anti-Catholic party no longer represented the timid opposition of a few malcontents, but, fed by material interest and protected by royal authority, grew into the great party of the Reformation in England. Henry was in no wise a conscious reformer. His regard for the Pope declined as his affection for Anne Boleyn increased. How he could have rejected papal authority, and at the same time have sought to maintain Catholic doctrine, is a mystery of religious purpose which baffles all attempts at successful analysis. The common-place law of self-interest solves the seeming paradox. Strange contrasts are found in the dealings of Tudor Royalty with the problems of the Reformation. Henry VIII and his progeny in turn cared nothing for toleration as a principle. Mary and Edward were fully convinced of their commission to do God's service. But Mary would have swept away the work of Edward had not her fierce zeal undermined the cause for which she would willingly have died. They differed as widely in their attitude to dissent as they differed in creed. Both were intolerant. But Mary was a persecutor.

Like the founder of her family, Elizabeth took up an independent political position between the two great powers, France and Spain. Like her father, she masqueraded in a garb of independence between the two great religions. She did not concern herself with dogma for its own sake. She never allowed her mental vision to fix itself upon the small points of doctrine, to the neglect of a broad general policy. Of the political unity which from the dawn of the Reformation was destined to supersede ecclesiastical unity among the Germanic speaking peoples, she could know or cared nothing. She turned from the Pope to her people for a vindication of her claims to legitimacy. The struggle between the Crown and the Puritans scarcely widened beyond the field of wordy ecclesiastical controversy. Puritanism was not yet a fighting force in England.

On the other hand, Elizabeth's strife with the Catholics represented a grave political exigency in which the perpetuity of her government, no less than Protestant establishment, was at stake. Justification of her deeds of blood, done under the impulse of political expediency, is a task which has never been accomplished by the most fulsome of Elizabeth's panegyrists. Three generations separated the Queen from the days of the undivided church. She was less hampered by tradition; she was called upon to make no violent break with the past. She looked upon Catholic intrigues as a challenge to royal authority, and met them with a policy of coercion which increased in severity until the day of her death.

Under James, the first of the Stuarts, the old policy of religious coercion was continued, but with the important distinction that Catholic and Puritan exchanged positions as objects of royal hostility. The political considerations which had armed Elizabeth against the Catholics, turned James and his successor with equal consistency against the Puritans. Precisely the causes which brought a relaxation of the penal laws against Catholics, induced increased severity toward the Puritans. The characteristic prejudice of the Puritan was his bigoted abhorrence of popery and prelacy. James' devotion to an erastian church is summed up in his favorite maxim—"No Bishop, no King." The struggle to preserve his autonomy took form in a contest with the Presbyterian clergy of Scotland before he came to the English throne. Melville, second only to Knox as a figure in Scottish ecclesiastical history, had assumed the leadership in a contest with the civil power, which culminated sixty years later in open rebellion against Charles I. Nor did the movement, essentially democratic, stay until it demanded the life of the King. Melville's doctrine of equality in things spiritual, imported from Geneva, and reared on the speculative basis that all laborers in Christ are equal, had been metamorphosed into the dogma of political equality. Political harangues from Scotch pulpits became the order of the day, James furnishing the mark for Presbyterian diatribes. The atrabilious humor of the Scotch clergy found expression in studied insults to the King. When Melville, plucking James by the sleeve, addressed him as "God's sillie vassall," he conveyed a volume of unwholesome truth to a sovereign transported with self-conceit and feverishly jealous of authority. James has recorded his experience at this period in his reply to Dr. Reynolds, at the Hampton Court conference: "If you aim," said he, "at a Scottish Presbytery, it agreeth as well with monarchy as God with the devil. Then Jack and Tom and Will and Dick shall meet and censure me and my council."

The democratic drift of Melville and his co-religionists had its genesis at Geneva—it was nourished in Scotland—extended across the border—spanned the ocean, and is read anew in the strife of the settlers on this spot for political equality. As the strength of the Puritan faction in England increased, the apparently irreconcilable parties of the opposition were drawn together for common defence. Long before Puritanism had gained absolute control in the overthrow and execution of Charles, the forces of the Court, the Established Church, the Catholics and the Arminians had practically joined hands against the common enemy. The hatred James bore to the Puritans, and his natural clemency to the Catholics, were further emphasized as early as 1616, when the King began negotiations for the "Spanish match." For seven years these negotiations for the marriage of Prince Charles to the Spanish Infanta dragged on through the tedious mazes of royal protocols and papal dispensations.

It was precisely within these years, when the penal laws against Catholics had been suspended, when scores of popish lords and knights were in the enjoyment of high public trusts, and the royal purpose pointed to a wider indulgence than had been known for half a century, that George Calvert projected his plan of western empire. As early as 1620, he had obtained title in Newfoundland for the purpose of "drawing back yearly some benefits therefrom." Not a scintilla of evidence goes to show that Calvert obtained this grant as an asylum for persecuted Catholics. Indeed, a considerable number of historians insist that Calvert was a Protestant when the grant was obtained. This plan of founding a Proprietary Colony for purposes of revenue only reached its development more than a decade later, when the charter of Maryland was penned. There was no break in policy or purpose. The Avalon venture proved a bad investment. When Calvert visited his Avalon plantation in 1627, he found the glowing pictures of its natural advantages highly overdrawn. The soil, alternately stiffened by frost and shadowed by fogs, banished all dreams of commercial success from this quarter. He writes a pitiful letter to King Charles, asking for a grant in Virginia, with such privileges as King James had been pleased to grant him. These privileges were granted in a charter modeled upon the Avalon patent. In their salient features the provisions of the two documents are identical. If it can not be insisted with reason that the Avalon colony was planted as a retreat for English Catholics, no more can the common opinion be justified that the Maryland grant was obtained with like design, unless it can be shown that a change of policy came with Calvert's supposed change of faith.

A host of authorities aver that George Calvert became a convert to the Catholic faith about the year 1624, after the planning of his Avalon Colony. This generally accepted theory rests in the last resort upon the testimony of two contemporary authorities—Fuller and Goodman. Thomas Fuller, Prebendary of Sarum, stamps on every page his violent anti-Catholic bias. The retirement of Calvert from the high office of Secretary of State, took place on the failure of the Spanish match in 1624. In this same year fifty-four eminent Catholics were dislodged from public office by an ultra-Protestant Parliament. The creed of every high officer of State was scrutinized as never before. Things suddenly recognized are often mistaken as things that have suddenly come into existence. Fuller's mistake in attributing Calvert's retirement from office to a supposed conversion to Catholicism was a natural one. The testimony of Dr. Thomas Goodman, Bishop of Gloucester, to the same effect bears internal evidence of inaccuracy. He avers that Calvert was converted by Gondomar, the Spanish Ambassador and the Earl of Arundel, whose daughter Calvert's son had married. When Gondomar was in England, Ann Arundel was a mere child, and could not have been married to Secretary Calvert's son. Furthermore, Arundel was not the man to make a successful missionary. It is not so much an open question as to whether he held this creed or that, but as to whether he thought it of sufficient importance to hold any creed at all.

In opposition to the commonly accepted theory of Calvert's conversion, may be set the testimony of reliable historians: Arthur Wilson plainly states that Calvert was a Catholic when first made Secretary of State in 1619. This was at least a year before his private scheme of western empire was mooted. Twice in connection with events which could not have occurred later than 1621, Calvert is classed with the adherents of the Church of Rome. Rapin, in his invaluable history, accepts the same view. Oldmixon speaks of Calvert as a popish secretary, in connection with an event which could not have transpired later than October, 1621, and in another work states, authoritatively, that Sir George Calvert was of the Romish religion when he obtained the grant in Newfoundland. Independent of direct testimony, the theory of Calvert's late conversion is untenable. King James bore no especial ill-will to life-long Catholics, but was intensely hostile to such as changed from the new faith to the old. Read the King's bitter tirades against such, and then consider his life-long regard for Calvert.

On the death of James, his son Charles desired to continue Calvert, who had now been raised to the peerage, a member of the Privy Council—offering at the same time to dispense with the oath of supremacy. Furthermore, the sudden conversion of Calvert introduces the dilemma of explaining the Catholic faith of all his progeny of whom we have any knowledge. Can it be assumed that they were trained as Protestants, and as suddenly as their father, abandoned the faith in which they had been reared?

It is reasonably certain that George Calvert was an adherent of the Church of Rome when advanced to the secretaryship. The whole fabric of his tardy conversion to Catholicism, and retirement from office in consequence, must fall to the ground. The public acknowledgment of his fidelity to the mother church is generally accepted as the cause of his withdrawal from power. It was simply a mask to cover his defeat by Buckingham. The divergent aims of the two in the Spanish match, and the ultimate triumph of Buckingham in his program of opposition, furnish conclusive evidence that Calvert's political career received its death-blow on the termination of friendly negotiations with the Spanish Court. Calvert had everything to gain in securing the marriage of Prince Charles to the Infanta. Sensitive in the highest degree to the breath of royal favor, he would naturally have bent every energy to accomplish the union upon which King James had set his heart. Aside from subservience to the wishes of the King, Calvert acted the more zealously in the matter, because of the wider indulgence in religion which the marriage would confer. For years, a warm support of the Spanish match was a passport to royal favor. The opposition of Nauton, the Protestant colleague of Calvert in the secretaryship, brought his downfall at an early stage of the proceedings. In the reaction which followed the utter defeat of the Spanish policy, Calvert himself was swept from power.

The Earl of Bristol was in full control of the negotiations with the Court at Madrid. But Calvert was the only Secretary employed in the Spanish match. The vigilance and penetration of Bristol were such that the most secret councils of the Spanish Court did not escape him. The King was more than satisfied; the accomplished Infanta was soon to arrive in England with a magnificent dowry, and assurance was given that the marriage would be the certain precursor of the restitution of the Palatinate. At this happy juncture Buckingham appears upon the scene. Among all the strong band of uncrowned heads, that his generation could marshal no man was more potential than he. His sway was more unlimited than had been that of Gaveston at the council board of the Plantagenet King, or of Essex at the Court of the Tudor Queen. His was the potency of a Sejanus, the unrivaled control of a Madam Pompadour. As is often the case with the low-born advanced to high station, Buckingham was proud, insolent, and excessively jealous of authority. Bristol's success in the negotiation with Spain was at once a challenge. A rival may be eclipsed by a greater light blazing in the same field, or crushed by direct personal attack. Buckingham determined to meet Bristol at Madrid, out-dazzle him in the eyes of the Spanish, out-bid him in the despatch of the royal commission. But not only did the favorite discover that the mine of popularity had been worked to its utmost capacity, but even found himself the peculiar object of the Spaniards' aversion. He changed his tactics. Burst into an open quarrel with Bristol over the ridiculous matter of precedence in a royal pleasure party. For weeks he employed his fruitless artifices to break the match which Bristol had negotiated, and finally succeeded by a preposterous demand that would have affronted any sovereign in Europe. An open rupture was inevitable. Wedding jewels were returned, and active preparations made for war. The Infanta tearfully resigned her short-lived title of Princess of Wales, and abandoned the study of the English language.

Buckingham returned to England the idol of the anti-Catholic party. In the day of his power his triumph was not complete while yet a Mordecai sat at the King's gate. Upon Middlesex, Bristol and Calvert, the trio of the opposition, the heavy hand of the low-born Favorite fell with blighting effect. Middlesex, who had "gained much credit with the King," during the Spanish negotiations, was stripped of public honors and thrust from his seat in the House of Lords. Bristol was flung into prison the day he set foot on native soil, and upon release, retired to private life. Both these men recognized the hand that smote them, as is abundantly shown by the records. The fate of Calvert, who, as late as January 14th, 1624, openly opposed in council a breach with Spain, could have been read in the fall of Middlesex and Bristol. "Mr. Secretary Calvert, writes a contemporary, hath never looked merrily since the Prince his coming out of Spain; it was thought he was much interested in the Spanish affairs; a course was taken to rid him of all employments and negotiations." "Secretary Calvert, says a letter written August, 1624, droops and keeps out of the way." Though driven from power by Buckingham, Calvert continued to enjoy the regard of King James and his son. He was created Baron of Baltimore, permitted to sell his Secretaryship, and left free to pursue those plans, on which his mind had been set for years, of empire beyond the sea. A decade of costly experiment closed with the grant of Maryland.

A grant, the "most ample and sovereign in its character that ever emanated from the English Crown."

George Calvert's son Cecilius, "heir to his father's intentions not less than to his father's fortunes," sent over his first colonists to Maryland in 1634. More than half of the members of the first expedition were Protestants. Out of two hundred and twenty, one hundred and twenty-eight on sailing refused the test oaths. Father More writes to Rome that "by far the greater part of the colony were heretics." Father White writes from the colony of St. Mary's, that of twelve who died from illness on the voyage, but two were Catholics. The Father Provincial laments in a letter to Rome that "three parts of the people, or four, at least, are heretics." Twenty years after the landing at St. Mary's, Hammond wrote that there were "but few papists in Maryland." While the first colony was numerically Protestant, Chancellor Kent is correct when he speaks of the colony as "the Catholic planters of Maryland," and Judge Story, when he says they "were chiefly Roman Catholics," and Bancroft, when he writes that the religious toleration of the early period of settlement was the work of Catholics. The physical balance of power was with the Protestants; the social, political and intellectual control was with the Catholics. Court records, council proceedings, the names given to towns, to Hundreds, to creeks, to manors, all offer testimony to Catholic control.

In bold relief above the portals of an arch at the Columbian Exposition is traced the inscription: "Toleration in Religion—the Best Fruit of the Last Four Centuries." The impartial verdict of history must concede to Calvert's Catholic colony the proud distinction of being the first, and, for a generation, the sole champion of religious freedom on the Western Hemisphere.

Controversy has centered about the famous Toleration Act of 1649. Protestants, as well as Catholics, have claimed the honor of its passage. The early religious freedom of which we boast had neither genesis nor supports in legislative enactments. Religious toleration prevailed as a habit of the settlers of St. Mary's, forceful and wholesome, as an inchoate law years before the hybrid statute of 1649 was submitted to vote. Unfriendly critics have further urged that this Catholic toleration had its genesis in political necessity, and was nurtured by a broad policy of far-sighted self-interest. We reject the unworthy imputation that the colonists of St. Mary's knew no higher sanction for their tolerance than the restrictions of a charter or the dictates of the common place law of self-interest. The course of history prior to the seventeenth century has been sufficient to show the irrelation between low ideals of conduct and religious persecution. Toleration was the child of force, not of philosophic calm. The mediaeval mind shaped action in countless instances to mean and unworthy ends, the mediæval heart sanctioned enormities of conduct which deeply tincture the annals of Europe with shameful and bloody revivals of lawlessness. Cruel and unusual punishments for wrong acts, as well as heretical opinions, are passing away. Sheep-stealing was punishable by death under the old English law. Wrong views of transubstantiation were met by the argument of the gibbet.

While all the homilies of two centuries have not sufficed to bring out a new moral truth, it must be borne in mind that moral standards are continually changing. We must look into the spirit of bygone times in order to appreciate the true worth and meaning of the great principle upheld by these settlers of St. Mary's. They had to suffer much, to surrender much, to obey, in the land of their nativity; with true nobility they welcome their former oppressors to their new found lands beyond the sea; with true nobility they pledge their officers not to molest any "person professing to believe in Jesus Christ for or in respect of religion." Whatever the motive, the world had not in that day seen the like.

As early as 1631, the government of the Virginia Colony became openly intolerant. Under the hand of Berkeley, the bigoted Church-of-England Governor, distress the most adverse fell upon the Puritan settlers on the Nansemond river. Under fire of persecution two Puritan elders fled to Maryland in 1648. It was probably at their suggestion that Governor Stone issued an invitation to the entire Nansemond church to cross over into Maryland. Stone's liberal promises of local self-government and freedom in religion stimulated the Puritan exodus from Virginia, and caused the refugees to indulge the dream of an independent colony in the new land of promise. At the outset they flatly refused to take the oath of allegiance. They haggled at the words "absolute dominion." And demurred at the obedience due Roman Catholic officers. For a year these refugees remained outside the pale of Baltimore's government, in the full determination to erect upon the shores of the Chesapeake a "Civitas Dei"—a church state, to which they gave the reverential name of "Providence." In 1651, they became again recalcitrant and refused to send delegates to the provincial assembly. They protested against the governor's hostile advance upon the Indians of the Eastern Shore. Stone regarded the act as rebellious, and required them to take the first oath of fidelity, on penalty of forfeiture of lands. The Puritans protested against the oath as repugnant to their consciences as Christians and contrary to their rights as free subjects of England. They denounced the power of the Lord Proprietor, for, said they, he is liable to make null that done in the "Assemblies for the good of the people." On notice by Stone that writs and warrants should no longer run in the name of the Commonwealth, but in that of the Lord Proprietor, the Puritans prepared for war. The gained a bloodless victory and summoned a legislative assembly. One of its first acts was the disfranchisement of Catholics. The act, though never rigidly enforced, has left an indelible stain upon their records. Both sides were now arming for a greater contest. The drama of Marston Moor was to be re-enacted in the New World. Questions were mooting far wider than the sphere of religious controversy. The principle of self-government and civil equality was at stake. The battle of the Severn was to determine whether the mediæval institution of a feudal principality should persist upon Maryland soil. The defeat of the royalists of St. Mary's was the vindication of the democratic principle in Maryland. Within a generation after the battle of the Severn, the Puritan settlement as a political aggregate had become a memory. At the restoration of monarchy in England, the Puritan combined with the more numerous Episcopalians and his less extreme brethren of Charles County, and completely lost his identity. Yet the last word of his movement has not yet been spoken. From the days of the Puritan challenge to the absolute authority of a feudal Lord, St. Mary's was doomed as the political centre of the

Province. Just two hundred years ago the theatre of the Puritan struggle received the name of "Annapolis," and was formally advanced to the political headship of the Province.

Three forms of relationships place us in communion with our fellows—the family, the State, property. Men have been slaves to all. To the family, as under the caste system of India; to the State, as under certain forms of the Spartan or Roman society; to property, as under the regime of the feudal middle ages. Christianity became the gateway of emancipation by teaching new lessons of the dignity and worth of man, and of his personal responsibility to God. Luther reiterated these half-forgotten truths. His was a reaction against the doctrine of corporate responsibility for opinion. The Protestant conception of individual responsibility to God has naturally given birth to a multitude of creeds and churches; all generically Protestant, because all are intolerant of the cardinal principle of the Roman Court, namely, allegiance to its authority. Yet it remained for these champions of self-magistracy in matters of faith to learn the first lesson in the practice of religious toleration from the Catholic settlers of Maryland.

Dr. Dexter in his History of Congregationalism, claims for Robert Browne, the leader of the ultra-Puritan Separatists, the proud distinction of being the first writer to state and defend, in the English tongue, the true and now accepted doctrine of the relation of the civil magistrate to the church. The voice of Browne was as of one crying in the wilderness; there was no practical application of his theories among his Puritan brethren, either in Geneva or England or Massachusetts or Maryland. Geneva is said to have been at once the strength and weakness of the Puritan. "His strength, because here he saw his ideal realized; his weakness, because it taught him to try to get his reforms through the State." Calvin instituted at Geneva a Theocracy, the like of which the world has never seen. It was not a State church, but a church State. For self-control was substituted State control—a control that became inquisitorial, exacting, unjust. Laced in by catechismal formularies, the free circulation of new ideas was impeded. The Puritan was the last to see the injustice of purging away heresy by the shedding of blood, he was the last to perceive the inadequacy of force to crush a man's opinions. He inclined a complacent ear to the dogma of exclusive salvation for those of his own sect— persecution followed as a corollary. In the years of Catholic toleration in Maryland, the question of religious toleration in Massachusetts was decided in the negative. Adverse opinions were exposed by the Synod of 1637, and in the white light of Puritan orthodoxy, and became heresies most foul. These Puritans had eaten of the bitter bread of persecution, they had sailed the seas and subdued the wilderness as victims of religious intolerance. When, however, they encountered a Quaker with wrong views—they proceeded to argue him into orthodoxy. Failing of this, they hung him. Intolerance and persecution do not stand upon the same plane. The one is rather a thing of necessity, consequent upon positiveness of opinion. The other is a thing of expediency. In our own day the power of the sword has happily departed from every form of religious opinion. This triumph is based on expediency rather than morality. Persecution does not neccessarily imply low ideals of conduct. The best Roman Emperors, as Trajan, Decius, Julian and Marcus Aurelius, were precisely those who singled out the early Christians for persecution. The extremest bigots, as St. Dominic, Carlo Borromeo, Calvin and Caraffa, have been men of the purest intentions and of unimpeachable morality. As doubt is the antecedent of new knowledge, so a spirit of intolerance is a necessary condition of progress. Men will not labor and incur sacrifice to discover the truth of subjects in respect to which they are perfectly content. John the Baptist, the uncouth proclaimer of a new dispensation, was intolerant—denouncing unsparingly the regime of the Scribe and Pharisee. Isaiah, that other great reproacher and mouth-piece of the desert, was intolcrant. Paul, the orthodox Jew of the polite world, with the inbreaking of the light becomes a "pestilent fellow and a mover of sedition." Only the person who holds that religious beliefs are essentially uncertain or essentially unimportant, can sweepingly condemn the religious intolerance of earlier ages. Persecution has few apologists and deserves none. We utterly condemn the narrowness of the persecuting Puritan, while acknowledging that it was a high, but not too great a price to pay for his splendid legacy to the cause of civil liberty. It was the political intolerance of the Puritan which overthrew the tyranny of hereditary power in England and in America. The Puritan who trod these walks boldly set about to redress the balance of the Old World—in the widening struggle for civil liberty. The spirit of the Puritan spoke again in the rejection of stamped paper. It flashed anew in the destruction of tea in yonder harbor. It echoed once more in the ban put upon the claims of great Eastern States to Western territory.

The toleration which rests upon respect for adverse opinion, lives on in the true courtesy of our citizens. For the nobility of a landed aristocracy, has been substituted among the sons of Maryland, the nobler title of the "grand old name of gentleman." The generation is now passing away which bore the griefs and devastations of a long and cruel war. In these years of peace, some have arisen who have never heard the call of grave political exigency; some who have never known the sacrifice for which a great public crisis pleads; some who may never understand the priceless worth of the free institutions under which they live, unless with heart aflame, they read the cost of liberty in the devoted hearts, the noble purpose, the spent lives of the generations that have gone before. Men sparing not themselves in years of eminent public service—men struggling to heal the awful breach between brethren—men relinquishing friends and fortune as the champions of an alien race—men placing their lives in pawn for their country's liberties. Such have been the sons of this Commonwealth, known in the councils of their State and nation. Honored of the world. Genius, nobleness, patriotism, have ever found a meeting place on this historic spot. The deeds of the men who have made us what we are, but mock the feeble breath of speech. Their work lives on, perpetuated by the strong men who even to-day gather within these historic walls.

> "Tho' much is taken, much abides; and tho'
> We are not now that strength which in old days
> Moved earth and heaven; that which we are, we are;
> One equal temper of heroic hearts,
> Made weak by time and fate, but strong in will
> To strive, to seek, to find, and not to yield."

LETTERS.

Much of the correspondence was incomplete or inappropriate to this volume. Such as was definite and pertinent has been inserted in this chapter.

ANNAPOLIS, *February 2, 1894.*

PROF. ALFRED P. DENNIS.

DEAR SIR:—It is my pleasant duty to inform you, that you have been unanimously chosen by the General Assembly of Maryland as orator, to represent it in the celebration to be had in this city, on the 5th day of March, 1894, of the removal of the Capital from St. Mary's to Annapolis. The celebration is under the control of the municipal authorities of Annapolis, and they will communicate with you in reference to the order of exercises and such other matters as may be necessary.

Yours respectfully,

THOMAS S. BAER,
Chairman of Committee on Public Records of House of Delegates.

PRINCETON, N. J., *February 9, 1894.*

HON. THOMAS S. BAER,

DEAR SIR:—I beg leave to acknowledge the receipt of your letter notifying me of my election as orator for the celebration of March 5th—and record my acceptance of the honor thus conferred. I trust you will pardon my delay. Have been confined in the College Hospital for ten days and could not earlier formulate a definite answer.

Most respectfully yours,
ALFRED P. DENNIS.

COUNCIL CHAMBER,
ANNAPOLIS, February 7, 1894.

JAMES W. THOMAS, ESQ.,

DEAR SIR:—I am instructed by the Committee of the City Council of Annapolis, to invite you to take part in our exercises on March 5th, in celebrating the 200th Anniversary of the "Removal of the Capital from St. Mary's to Annapolis," by reading a paper on St. Mary's City.

You have been assigned to the exercises of the afternoon at St. John's College.

I have handed this note over to Dr. Fell, President of St. John's College, who will further communicate with you.

Very respectfully,
ELIHU S. RILEY.

ST. JOHN'S COLLEGE,
PRESIDENT'S ROOM,
ANNAPOLIS, MD., *7th February, 1894.*

JAMES H. THOMAS, ESQ.,

MY DEAR SIR:—By request of Mr. E. S. Riley, the City Counsellor, I have the pleasure to hand you the enclosed invitation to deliver an address on St Mary's, on the occasion of the celebration of the removal of the Capital from that city to Annapolis.

As it is suggested that your address or paper, on the subject mentioned, be delivered in the afternoon of the 5th March, and shall form part of the program of the exercises, more particularly connected with the college, I write to say that we shall be much pleased to accord you a place in our program, following the address of General H. Kyd Douglas, upon King William's School.

It is proposed that the exercises shall commence about 4 o'clock P. M., in McDowell Hall, on Monday, the 5th March.

Trusting that you may be willing to accept the invitation, and to accord with the arrangement just mentioned,

I am, very respectfully yours,

THOMAS FELL,
President of St. John's College.

CUMBERLAND, MD., *February 10th, 1894.*

DR. THOMAS FELL,

ANNAPOLIS, MD.,

DEAR SIR:—I have the honor to acknowledge the receipt of your esteemed favor of the 8th inst., conveying a communication from the committee of the City Council of Annapolis, requesting me to deliver an address on "St. Mary's City," the early metropolis and capital of Maryland, on the occasion of the celebration of the 200th anniversary of Annapolis as the capital of the State.

It will give me pleasure to participate in that interesting ceremony, and to make a brief address upon the historic, but the vanished and almost forgotten, city of St. Mary's.

In thus conveying my acceptance through you to Mr. E. S. Riley, of the City Council, I beg also to express my appreciation of the courtesies extended by you in that connection as President of St. John's College.

Yours very respectfully,

JAMES W. THOMAS.

HEADQUARTERS MEADE POST No. 27, G. A. R.,

ANNAPOLIS, MD., *March 2, 1894.*

ELIHU S. RILEY, ESQ.,

DEAR SIR:—Your kind invitation to this Post to take part in the parade, Monday, March 5, 1894, to celebrate the Two Hundredth Anniversary of the Removal of the Capital of Maryland to Annapolis, received, and the Adjutant was directed to answer the same, informing your Honorable Body of the peculiar condition that exists in this Post which would make it almost impossible to attend in a body. Secondly, there are those of our members who are so employed that it would be impossible for them to participate. Wishing the celebration much success and beautiful weather,

I am, very respectfully,

Your obedient servant,

L. B. SMITH,

Adjutant Meade Post No. 27, G. A. R.

---

61 GLOUCESTER STREET,

ANNAPOLIS, MD., *February 20th, 1894.*

DEAR SIR:—I regret being unable to accept your courteous invitation for next Monday, having several days ago made arrangements to fulfil two important engagements in Baltimore on that day.

I have long felt deeply interested in the history and prosperity of "My Maryland," and most heartily wish you a successful celebration of your Metropolitan Centennial.

   Believe me, dear sir,
     Yours cordially,
       DECATUR V. B. MORGAN.

To ELIHU S. RILEY, ESQ.,
  Counsellor at Law,
   Court House, Annapolis.

      February, 21st, 1894.

ELIHU S. RILEY, ESQ.,
  ANNAPOLIS, MD.

DEAR SIR:—I am directed by the gentlemen of the Council of the Society of Colonial Wars in the State of Maryland, to thank your Committee, through you, for their courteous invitation for this Society to participate in the Bi-Centennial of the Removal of the Capital to the city of Annapolis, and to convey the acceptance of the invitation by the Society. Will you kindly inform me, by return mail, of the time and place of meeting and formation, and such details of the ceremonies as it may be convenient for you to communicate.

   Very respectfully yours,
     GEO. NORBURY MACKENZIE.

ANNAPOLIS, *March 2, 1894.*

ELIHU S. RILEY, ESQ.,

DEAR SIR:—I accept with pleasure the duty assigned to me by the Committee of Arrangements, of making the opening prayer at the celebration next Monday evening.

Yours sincerely,

WM. SCOTT SOUTHGATE.

PALESTINE COMMANDERY NO. 7.

ANNAPOLIS, *February 27, 1894.*

JOS. S. M. BASIL, JR., ESQ.,

Assistant Marshal.

MY DEAR SIR:—In reply to your invitation extended to our Commandery, would say, that it being impossible to obtain dispensation, Palestine Commandery must decline same.

Wishing your procession much success and a fine day.

I am, courteously yours,

RICH'D H. GREEN.

Recorder.

HALL OF ST. MARY'S BAY COUNCIL, NO. 175,
CATHOLIC BENEVOLENT LEGION,

ANNAPOLIS, *February 28th, 1894.*

SIR:—I am in receipt of the committee's invitation to this council to participate in the procession on the 5th proximo.

In reply, I beg to state, that this council, at its last meeting, decided to decline to participate, owing to the inability of the majority of its members to be absent from duty on that day.

   Very truly, &c.,

    For the Council, RASMUS CLAUSEN,

          Secretary.

MR. J. S. M. BASIL, JR.,

  Assistant Marshal.

      BALTIMORE, *February 24, 1894.*

MR. ELIHU S. RILEY,

 For the Committee on Celebration, etc.,

     Council Chamber, Annapolis.

DEAR SIR:—I have the honor to acknowledge, on behalf of the Maryland Historical Society, the reception of your communication of the 14th inst., addressed to its president, inviting the Society to participate in the procession to take place in your city on the 5th March, to celebrate the Two Hundredth Anniversary of the Removal of the Capital to Annapolis.

It is a matter of much regret that there will be no meeting of the Society before your anniversary, at which this invitation can be presented for the Society's action.

I beg, however, in advance of such presentation, to express to you and the committee you represent, the thanks of the Society for your recollection of it in your arrangements for the celebration. In the absence of the opportunity for more formal action by the Society, two of its officers will be requested to be present and represent it on the occasion.

I am, sir, very truly yours,

MENDES COHEN,
Corresponding Secretary.

ANNAPOLIS, MD., *March 2d, 1894.*

MR. E. S. RILEY, ESQ.,

DEAR SIR:—We have received your invitation to participate in the parade on Monday, 5th inst., and regret to say that we will not be able to do so, as the time required to get the members together and make the necessary arrangements are too short. We can not have another meeting for two weeks.

Very respectfully,

E. H. SAMUELS,
Post Commander, Sheridan Post, G. A. R.
C. H. SMITH, *Adjutant.*

The following congratulatory greetings were sent on the occasion to St. John's College:

UNITED STATES NAVAL ACADEMY.

March 3, 1894.

Your invitation for the Academic Board to meet the Board of Visitors of St. John's College, at 3.45 P. M., March 5th, and proceed with them to take part in the celebration of the Bi-Centenary of King William's School, has been laid before the Board, and it will give them pleasure to accept the same.

C. H. CHESTER,
Commander U. S. Navy, Commanding.

JOHNS HOPKINS UNIVERSITY.

BALTIMORE, MD., *March 5th, 1894.*

In the absence of the President of the Johns Hopkins University, the Academic Council sends its congratulations to the Visitors and Governors of St. John's College on the occasion of the Bi-Centenary of an institution that has done memorable service to the cause of education in this State, with best wishes for increased prosperity and usefulness.

IRA REMSEN, Sec'y.

JOHNS HOPKINS UNIVERSITY.

BALTIMORE, MD., *March 5th, 1894.*

Let me congratulate you upon the interesting historic anniversary which you are now celebrating. Kindly accept this word from the Historical Department as a token of rejoicing with you in the honorable record of St. John's College.

H. B. ADAMS,

Prof. Hist.

JOHNS HOPKINS UNIVERSITY.

BALTIMORE, MD., *March 5th, 1894.*

I am sorry not to be present at your Bi-Centenary. I am greatly disappointed. I send congratulations to you on the auspicious circumstances under which you celebrate this interesting anniversary.

EDWARD H. GRIFFIN,

Dean.

THE WOMAN'S COLLEGE OF BALTIMORE, MD.

March 3d, 1894.

The President and Faculty of the Woman's College send greeting to St. John's College.

Professor Wm. H. Hopkins will attend the exercises on March 5th, as a delegate from the Woman's College.

BALTIMORE CITY COLLEGE.

March 5th, 1894.

I regret that our duties here will probably prevent the attendance of myself and colleagues. We wish you a most successful occasion.

F. A. SOPER,
Principal.

THE BISHOP OF MARYLAND,

RT. REV. WM. PARET, B. A.

I regret much that my duties and positive engagements will not permit me to be present at the 200th Anniversary of King William's School. You have my hearty wishes and prayers for still longer and stronger life work. And I beg you to assure the Board of Trustees of my interest in the College, and my wish that I could have found it possible to be present.

WILLIAM PARET,
Bishop of Maryland.

CARDINAL ARCHBISHOP OF BALTIMORE.

BALTIMORE, MD., *February 28th, 1894.*

The Cardinal Archbishop of Baltimore regrets that his Lenten duties will deprive him of the pleasure of attendance on the occasion of the Bi-Centenary of King William's School.

CARDINAL ARCHBISHOP OF BALTIMORE.

REV. LEIGHTON PARKS, D. D.
of Emanuel Church, Boston.

March 3, 1894.

I trust that the celebration will be the success that it deserves, and that the future of the college may be bright and prosperous.

LEIGHTON PARKS.

REV. F. J. KEECH, M. A.

NEW YORK CITY, *March 5, 1894.*

Accept my hearty good wishes for continued and renewed prosperity of my alma mater upon this its Bi-Centenary Celebration.

F. J. KEECH.

ANNAPOLIS IN 1694.

After forty-five years of growth, Annapolis, in 1694, had under forty houses in it, and, it may be estimated, not over one hundred and fifty inhabitants. Within its precincts and in its vicinity were names that have linked themselves with every stage of progress of the "Old Line State." From the ancient rent-rolls are taken the names of the men who first settled in Annapolis and its vicinity, and whose posterity lived in Annapolis when it became the Capital of the State, with here and there some sturdy son of the virgin settlement who remained to see the steady progress and new honors of "the Ancient City." The dates show the years when the surveys were made and the land taken up for patent.

    RICHARD BENNETT, 1650.
    THOMAS GOTT, 1658.
    WILLIAM GALLOWAY, 1659.
    JOHN COLIER, 1659.
    SAMUEL RUTHERS, 1661.

In Middle Neck Hundred, between Severn and South Rivers:

    ZEPHENIAH SMITH, 1650.
    MATTHEW HOWARD, 1650.
    WM. CROUCH, 1650.
    JOHN HOWARD, 1650.

RICHARD WARFIELD, 1650.
ALEX. WARFIELD, 1650.
THOMAS TODD, 1651.
JAMES HOMES, 1651.
ANN OWEN, 1684.
NICH. WYAT, 1651.
SAM. DORSEY.
RICHARD ACTON, 1651.
PETER PORTER, 1651.
JOHN BALDWIN, 1661.
CHRISTOPHER OATLY, 1651.
RICHARD BEARD, 1650.
THOMAS HOWELL, 1651.
WILLIAM HOMES, 1652.
JAMES WARNER, 1651.
HENRY PINKNEY, 1651.
THOS. GATES, 1658.
JOHN HOWARD, 1658.
WILLIAM GALLOWAY, 1659.
TOBIAS BUTLER, 1659.
NEAL CLARK, 1659.
GEO. LAUGHER, 1650.
SAML. WHITERS, 1661.
LAWRENCE RICHARDSON, 1661.
ANN CORELL, 1661.
EDWARD HOPE, 1661.
COL. HENRY RIDGELY, 1661.
CHARLES RIDGELY, 1661.
JACOB BENINGTON, 1661.
WILLIAM FRIZZELL, 1663.

NEAL CLARK, 1663.
EDWARD SKIDMORE, 1662.
NICHOLAS WYAT, 1662
CORNELIUS HOWARD, 1662.
SAML. HOWARD, 1662.
JOHN HOWARD, 1662.
CHARLES STEPHENS, 1662.
WALTER SMITH, 1662.
JOHN EDWARDS, 1662.
PATRICK DUNKAN, 1663.
JOHN HOWARD, 1663.
CHARLES STEPHENS, 1663.
RALPH SALMON, 1663.
JOHN JAMES, 1663.
HENRY SEWELL, 1663.
THOMAS UNDERWOOD, 1663.
EDWARD DORSEY, 1663.
JOHN DORSEY, 1663.
JOSHUA DORSEY, 1663.
CORNELIUS HOWARD, 1663.
JOHN EDWARDS, 1663.
RICHARD MOSS, 1663.
THOMAS HAMMOND, 1664.
WILLIAM GUMES, 1664.
WILLIAM READ, 1665.
JOHN C. MACCUBIN, 1665.
ROBERT CLARK, 1664.
THOMAS ROPER, 1664.
JOHN BARTON, 1665.
THOMAS BELL, 1665.

In Broad and Town Neck Hundred, between Severn and Magothy Rivers:

ROBERT BIRLE, 1650.
ABRAM HOLMAN, 1650.
RICHARD EWEN, 1652.
THOMAS HOMWOOD, 1652.
LEWIS JONES, 1652.
JOSHUA MERIKEN, 1652.
RICHARD YOUNG, 1652.
JOHN COWELL, 1651.
WILLIAM DURAND, 1651.
RALPH HAWKINS, 1652.
JAMES HOMEWOOD, 1652.
NATH. UTIE, 1658.
WILLIAM HOPKINS, 1659.
PHILIP HOWARD, 1659.
EDWARD LLOYD, 1659.
JAMES RIGBY, 1659.
WILLIAM FULLER, 1659.
ELIZABETH STRONG, 1659.
MATTHEW CLARK, 1659.
HENRY CATLINS, 1659.
THOMAS BROWN, 1659.
HENRY WOOLCHURCH, 1662.
WILLIAM PYTHER, 1659.
RICHARD DEVAIER, 1662.
MATTHEW HOWARD, 1663.
ALICE DURAND, 1662.
ROBERT TAYLOR, 1662.
ABRAM DAWSON, 1662.

WILLIAM LLOYD, 1662.
THOMAS TURNER, 1662.
ROBERT LUSBY, 1662.
EDWARD SKIDMORE, 1663.
ROBERT TYLER, 1663.
SARAH MARSH, 1663.
THOMAS C. MARSH, 1663.
JOHN ASKEW, 1663.
JOHN GREEN, 1663.
WILLIAM STAID, 1662.
JOHN HAMMOND, 1663.
EMMANUELL DREW, 1663.
ELIZABETH DARRELL, 1663.
CHRISTIAN MERRIKEN, 1665.
THOMAS THURSTON, 1664.
THOMAS COLE, 1664.
WILLIAM HILL, 1665.
JAMES ORWICK, 1665.
RICHARD MOSSEN, 1665.
RICHARD DEVOUR, 1662.
JOHN BROWN, 1665.
JOHN CLARK, 1665.
HERMAN SOLLING, 1665.
ELIZABETH HILLS, 1666.
GEORGE YATE, 1666.
ROBERT PETTYBON, 1666.
EDWARD BLAY, 1666.
JOHN ROCKHOLD, 1666.
PAUL DORRELL, 1667.
MORRICE BAKER, 1667.
JAMES CONNAWAY, 1668.

GEO. NORMAN, 1669.
JOHN BURTON, 1667.
WILLIAM DAWS, between 1667 and 1670.
WILLIAM READ, 1665.
HENRY PIERPONT, 1665.
PHILLIP THOMAS, 1664.
WALTER PHELPS, 1665.
NICHOLAS GREEN, 1665.
FRANCIS REASLY, 1666.
ELIZABETH SISSON, 1666.
WILLIAM HARRIS, 1667.
JEANE SISSON, 1667.
EDWARD DORSEY, 1668.
THOMAS PHELPS, 1668.
WILLIAM HOPKINS, 1669.
GUY MEEK. 1669.
RICHARD WARFIELD, 1669.
EDWARD GARDNER, 1669.

ANNAPOLIS IN 1894.

In 1845, Annapolis had, after nearly two hundred years of growth, increased to 3,000 inhabitants. The Naval Academy gave it a slight impetus when it was established there at the last-named date, and Annapolis in 1890 was reported as having over 7,000 souls. This does not include the Naval Academy and residents adjacent to the town, which would make the number nearly 9,000.

Dignified with the seat of government in 1694, Annapolis had put on its honors with the stir of a new vitality. Its name was changed to its present one from Ann Arundel Town, ship yards were laid out, a parish church (the present St. Anne's parish and now the third church), a schoolhouse (King William's School, now St. John's College), and a public ferry over the Severn, which was maintained until 1887, when it was superseded by a bridge, followed each other in rapid order.

The city of Annapolis has not made progress in wealth nor in population, but its development, on better lines, has been the pride of its people. With the arrival of the capital and a new element, came politicians, lawyers, legislators, judges and scholars. Here grace and beauty gathered, and in this prototype of an English capital, wealth, leisure, beauty and refinement created a life of social gayety and voluptuous enjoyment that made the city famous throughout all the colonies for its fastidious pleasures, whilst the culture and elegance of its people gained for it the title of "The Athens of America." Nor was the title undeserved. From its civilization were evolved Charles Carroll of Carrollton, Charles Wilson Peale, William Pinkney, Daniel Dulaney, Reverdy Johnson and John D. Godman, in the last century, and in the present, Stewart Holland, the hero of the Arctic; James Booth Lockwood, of the Greeley expedition; Stuart Robson, representative of the histrionic art; Dennis W. Mullan, the hero of Samoa—all of whom were born in Annapolis—and many others in both eras whose names belong to the history of the whole country.

The spirit, character and patriotism of the people of Annapolis are written in deeds like these: The battle of the Severn, 1656; establishment of King William's School, 1696; founding of the Gazette, 1727; the merciful reception of the banished Acadians, 1755; erection of the first theater in America, in 1760; mobbing of Hood, the stamp act tax gatherer in 1765; the burning of the Peggy Stewart and her tea in 1774; furnishing two incidents in the bill of indictment of George III, in the Declaration of Independence: mobbing the Tories of 1812, who dared rejoice by a sermon and procession over the fall of Napoleon and the freeing of English legions to fight America, and in gaining the love of Washington next to his Mount Vernon home.

The people of the "Ancient City" today, inheritors of the same blood, are legatees of the same spirit that characterized their forefathers, and are noted for their intelligent grasp of vital issues and their fearless vindication of their free-born rights.

NOTES, INCIDENTS, THANKS.

Among the representatives of the Maryland Historical Society taking part in the civic and military procession, was Edwin Warfield, Esq., of Howard county, who is a lineal descendant of Major Edward Dorsey, who represented Ann Arundel county in the Legislature of 1694.

In the House of Delegates of 1894, is Ormond Hammond, Esq., of Talbot county, who is a lineal descendant of Capt. John Hammond, who represented Ann Arundel county in the Legislature of 1694.

Fenton Lee Duvall, one of the ushers at the Hall of House of Delegates, on March 5, is a lineal descendant of Gov. Thomas Johnson, of Maryland, who nominated Gen. Washington to be commander of the Army and Navy of the thirteen united colonies.

John R. and Peter H. Magruder, ushers, March 5, are lineal descendants of Gov. Francis Nicholson.

All of the four speakers, on the occasion of the celebration, were Protestants, so the historical facts, recited by them, were not colored by religious bias.

Nicholas Brewer, one of the Board of Visitors and Governors of St. John's College, and one of the committee of arrangements, is a descendant of Nicholas Brewer, who gathered the boats together for Washington to cross the Delaware, the night he captured the Hessians.

Senator Washington Wilkinson, of St. Mary's, is a descendant of Rev. William Wilkinson, rector of Poplar Hill Protestant Episcopal Church, in 1650, the first Episcopal church in Maryland.

Col. Casperus A. Herman, delegate from Cecil county, in 1694, built the first State House at Annapolis, in 1696.

Elihu S. Riley, historian of the celebration, is a lineal descendant of Col. Henry Ridgely, the major of the armed troop of Anne Arundel in 1661, for the defense of the colony.

Dr. Abram Claude, one of the ex-mayors of Annapolis, who took part in the parade, is the grandson of Mr. Abraham Claude, who, with other citizens of Annapolis, in August, 1765, successfully resisted here the landing of Hood, the stamp-tax collector.

Charles H. Carter, Esq., member of the House, from the Second Legislative District of Baltimore, 1894, is a descendant of Lord Baltimore.

The masquerade procession was attended by a singular accident. Mr. John Gates was crossing West street, extended, on horseback, when Mr. Frank Small came up the street on another horse at a full gallop; the horses collided. Small's horse was killed outright, and Gates' died shortly afterward. Both riders were injured and knocked senseless. Gates recovered consciousness in thirty minutes; Small remained in a comatose condition for several hours. The former was only slightly injured; Small was seriously hurt, but finally recovered.

THANKS OF THE CITY COUNCIL OF ANNAPOLIS.

In the City Council of Annapolis, on March 12, 1894, on motion of City Counsellor Riley, it was—

Ordered, That the thanks of the City Council are hereby tendered to Allan McCullough, Esq., Chief Marshal, Mr. J. S. M. Basil, Jr., First Assistant Marshal, and the Assistant Marshals, for the faithful performance of all the duties assigned them in the procession of March 5th. Also, to all the organizations that assisted in forming the line of the procession, and to our citizens generally, whose hearty co-operation made the celebration exercises a marked success.

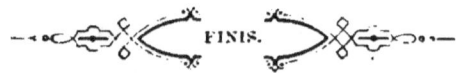

www.ingramcontent.com/pod-product-compliance
Lightning Source LLC
Chambersburg PA
CBHW020253170426
43202CB00008B/345